P9-DWW-637

# Granny Is My Wingman

# Granny Is
# My Wingman

## Kayli Stollak

*New Harvest*
*Houghton Mifflin Harcourt*
BOSTON • NEW YORK

*Library of Congress Cataloging-in-Publication Data*
Stollak, Kayli.
Granny is my wingman / Kayli Stollak.
pages  cm
ISBN 978-0-544-11452-4
1. Online dating. I. Title.
HQ801.82.S76 2013
306.730285 — dc23
2013010499


Printed in the United States of America
DOC 10 9 8 7 6 5 4 3 2 1

Author's Note: I have changed the names and identifying characteristics of
some of the individuals featured throughout this book to protect their pri-
vacy, and in a few instances composite characters based entirely on real people are used.

*For Granny*

# Contents

# Granny Is My Wingman

# Who the *Hell* Is Jenna Jones?!

**M**Y FRENEMY FROM seventh grade got married over the weekend to a man who wears neon sunglasses. The boy I lost my virginity to donated blood and three of his friends liked it. The douchey guy from my freshman sociology class is listening to Rihanna on Spotify.

And I was lying in bed on a Monday morning lurking around Facebook like a big old creep. Thanks to Mark Zuckerberg I spent a lot of mornings like this. I scrolled through countless pictures of "friends" and virtual strangers, while I lightly humped my comforter, wrapping it tight between my legs. It was a weird maneuver that had become second nature to me over the past year. Who needs a man when you have a duvet? Sure, it didn't cuddle back, but it kept me cozy and hadn't broken up with me yet, so I felt pretty good about the relationship.

It was a warm summer morning on the Lower East Side of Manhattan. Actually, it was 12:30 p.m., which to most functioning individuals would be considered afternoon. Not me! As a twenty-four-year-old paying off my student loans by running around a nightclub doling out bottles of booze, opening my eyes to the world before 1 p.m. was a major accomplishment.

I grabbed my pillow and stuffed it tight against my chest. Oh boy, did I miss the days when there was an actual human lying beside me. I'd crawl onto his chest. We'd spoon. Sometimes I would even be the big spoon. Spooning a man who is a foot taller than you—that is love. That *was* love.

Nope, none of that was going down in my apartment anymore. Instead I was busy distracting myself by looking at the carefully curated lives of other people. Catching up on their Foursquare check-ins and broadcasted humble brags like it was my goddamn job.

Two years earlier, when I graduated from New York University with a degree in filmmaking, I assumed I was on a straightforward trajectory. Before finishing school I locked down a steady job working for a production company that made commercials. I had been on track to a solid career until I gave it all up last year when the advertising world started to feel less like an artistic outlet and more like bullshit.

Rather than look for another job in film production (the field that I took out nearly $200,000 in student loans to get a degree in), I decided to pick up more shifts as a cocktail waitress in the swanky club I had been working at since college. I wasn't a fan of rich assholes, catty girls, or high heels—but, I could work three nights a week, take two months of vacation, and still make nearly $100,000 a year.

There was also my boyfriend's departure back to London, which may have had some influence on my career decision. I suddenly didn't have the pressure to grow up, work in an office, or prepare to procreate—the club, the antithesis of adult life, where "work" is essentially hanging out with friends while drinking expensive champagne, seemed like the best option.

Back to Monday, I had a hangover and *owed* it to myself to flop around in bed. I was on the verge of working up the strength to exit the soul-sucking social network and award myself with a bagel when I saw *it*. My heart lurched, my breath caught in my chest, my fists clenched into little balls of granite. "Who the *fuck* is Jenna Jones?!" I screamed at my computer screen.

Huang, my Craigslist roommate, popped his tiny head into my bedroom, his hands half-covering his eyes. "Uh, you okay?" he whispered.

"Yeah, yup, uh huh," I tried to respond. "Actually, you know what? Can you get out of here?"

He nodded, scurrying across the hall to his room. Huang and I were not close; in fact we barely talked. He moved in as a subletter a year earlier when Charlie, my ex, moved back across the pond. Before Huang, Charlie and I had impromptu dance parties in the kitchen, rollerbladed in the living room, and boned on every available surface.

Now it was just me and Huang cohabiting in my former love den. It was supposed to be temporary, but Huang ended up sticking around. We never did the bonding thing, probably because he moved in during the time of tearful meltdowns, Adele on repeat, and a revolving door of friends coming in for weepy couch confessions.

Poor Huang, he never knew if the moans coming from my bedroom were from crying or masturbating.

A note on the politics of Facebook: I know it's not healthy to stalk exes. That's why *I* defriended him after we broke up, specifically to avoid moments like these. But it popped up in my goddamn news feed anyway: a picture his sister posted of them. Several pictures actually, several disgustingly adorable pictures that I considered clicking "report" on so Facebook would take them down.

There was one of Jenna Jones wearing the protective leather catsuit his mother had passed down to *me* for motorcycle trips. And she was holding a helmet, was it *my* helmet? The helmet I had painted, in gold-and-pink sparkly letters, LOVE TOWN: POP. 2 on the back of for our first trip to Spain? Motorcycle adventures were *our* thing. Now it was *their* thing. There it was. I didn't need to look any further (or get one of my friends who was still "friends" with him to snoop out his current "relationship status") to know what was up. This was serious. A status had been changed; he was declaring his relationship publicly on Facebook and his new gal was a perfect fit for my leather onesie.

I knew this day would come. I even suspected he was seeing someone, but now there was this cold, hard evidence in my feed. Why didn't I think to defriend all of his friends and family? (The obvious answer: I'm a masochistic stalker.) There were pictures of Jenna Jones with his mom and dad at their farm where we stayed together countless times. Pictures of him laughing with the wench. Take off my goddamn pants, Jenna Jones! I summoned a satanic *Exorcist* voice. "Who is she? Who is she? Who is she?" I chanted.

Okay, fine, I knew who she was. She was the girl who he was moving on with. She was the one who fit the mold, the one who would give him everything I could not.

# Hitting Is a Part of Healing

"YOU CAN SLAP ME if you want to," Charlie said the last time I saw him.

I knew he was kidding but I couldn't let the opportunity slip away. It was petty, but slapping him was *exactly* what I wanted. It was really over. We had broken up almost a year prior and since we lived in different countries, we were doing a generally good job of keeping our distance. Still, after we ended things, I made a couple of trips across the Atlantic, during which sexual acts were committed and, far worse, loving words exchanged. We had been stringing each other along, but not anymore. This was it. He was starting to date; he had just turned thirty-six and was ready for all the grown-up things that I would never share with him.

At twenty-four, I was standing on a cobblestone street in London, the city I was supposed to be living in, facing the man who was supposed to be mine. The reality of the end finally hit me, unironically, like a slap in the face. I took a deep breath, trying to soothe the knot in my stomach and the tightening in my chest. Somehow over the past year, in my stages of grief over our failed love, I managed to avoid the notion that we would never end up together.

I felt sick with fury, my face shamelessly dripping with tears. Resentment rose up inside of me. He didn't want to be with me—it wasn't a crime, but it felt like he was killing me. If breaking up is a grieving process, then I'd definitely reached anger and had the fun steps of bargaining and depression to look forward to.

With wet eyes we faced each other on Shoreditch High Street, smiling, knowing that even though the end was ugly, the beginning and middle were so wildly beautiful. Then with swift force I took my right hand to his left cheek. We stood there in silence, shocked by my act of physical violence. My slap was immature, only delivering a brief, inconsequential pain; yet it was still a way to hurt him, even for just a moment. We wiped the tears from each other's faces, hugged, and parted ways. And that was it.

The end felt oddly similar to the beginning. Our story opened and closed on the street. It all caught up with us as we always suspected it would. It began on my turf, in my country, in my city of New York. We met on Labor Day weekend in 2006, just a few days before my sophomore year of NYU began. He was English, visiting the city for the weekend to attend a friend's wedding. At the time, he was in his early thirties, with enough facial scruff to make a young gal hot under the collar.

Sitting on the curb outside my Lower East Side apartment on Ludlow Street, I spotted him drinking a take-out margarita from El Sombrero, the cheap Mexican restaurant on the corner. My roommate and I had just purchased a heavy armoire for twenty dollars from a crackhead on Bowery and wooed a man driving by in a van to drop it off in front of our building. It was perfect for our cluttered apartment, but there was no way we were getting it up our seven-story walk-up.

I was nineteen, busty, brassy, and full of confidence. I tugged my tank top down to reveal a couple of extra inches of cleavage as I sauntered up to him and his friend. "You guys like beer?" I purred, trying my best to summon the sexual prowess of a woman *at least* twenty-two. They looked up from their margaritas, shading their eyes from the sun, nodding enthusiastically.

"Cool, come upstairs, we've got a pack of Coronas." I smiled. Sure, "normal" girls wouldn't lure strange men into their home with promises of alcohol, but we were hell-bent on taking in every spontaneous moment our city had to offer. It was summer and we were nineteen and living out a 24/7 party fantasy.

The men looked puzzled but pleased—thoughts of college-style porno plots must have been running through their thirty-year-old heads. "But first could you carry this armoire up for us?" I pointed toward my roommate, who was leaning seductively against the wardrobe, twirling her golden locks.

They foolishly agreed. Watching them struggle with the armoire, but still trying to impress us young, giggly girls while they made it up the seven steep flights into our shoebox apartment was one of the funniest moments of my life. We cracked open beers as the boys eyed our freakshow home. It was a disaster zone littered with glittery tops, pictures of us covered in brownie batter, a Paris Hilton sex tape, and a gigantic dildo someone gave us which sat on top of our TV stand like the patron saint of Ludlow Street.

"Now what?" Charlie asked.

Our eyes met, our connection was effortless and immediate. "We get weird," I replied. And so it began. We spent the rest of the day and night together, bouncing from Max Fish to Sweet and Vicious to Epstein's to Dark Room, sharing our stories, sense of humor, passion, drinks, and wacky dance moves.

We clicked so intensely but we both feared the inevitable. Besides the fact that he was leaving town in the morning, he was twelve years older than me (despite what my fake ID said) and lived on a different continent.

As the sun came up, we sat in my bed eating Cheerios and drinking beer, counting the hours until he'd have to board a plane and fly back to London. We decided it would be best to write it off as a fling. But I was young and he was reckless and we couldn't let it go.

A string of hilarious emails led to a series of wild adventures. There were motorcycle trips across Europe, trekking through Guatemala, music festivals in Spain. It was all so spontaneous, wild, and romantic. But long distance can't sustain forever.

Out of love, we made huge gestures and sacrifices to keep our relationship afloat. We chased each other back and forth across the Atlantic, taking turns spending six months at a time in the other's country, trying to find a balance and pick a home base. Luckily once I graduated, both of us could make a living in either New York or London—he was a writer and could do that anywhere and I worked for a production company that had offices in both countries—but we each felt an allegiance to our own city.

When he turned thirty-five the looming problems that we had foreseen came to term. His paternal clock started ticking and his career took off. He wanted to stick with his work in England, be closer to his family and friends, and ultimately settle down.

I was only a year out of college. I knew I wanted to be with him but I didn't know when I would be ready to have a ring on my finger or a baby in my belly. I was only beginning to get into my New York grown-up groove.

He left for London in the winter of 2010 and I was to follow permanently in the spring. I tried charging ahead: I started my visa process and did my best to adjust to the idea of working full time in an English production office. I even began to convince myself that I could have kids in the next year or two and that I would be happy living in the country-side.

As the seasons changed, the distance between us worked to sober us up from our love-drunk illusions. He began to pull away from me and find any reason for a fight. Neither of us ever cheated or wronged the other in any real way, but we were growing up and entering different phases of our lives that we couldn't fairly journey on together. Our expiration date had arrived.

Bitter emails, uncomfortable Skype chats, and tear-filled phone calls took over our relationship. At the risk of sounding über cliché, thus far in my existence he was the love of my life, and I was terrified that I was losing my one chance to experience that kind of epic love. I relentlessly clung to the idea of the fun, adoring guy who I met on the sidewalk, the guy who made love to me doggy style at a monastery on top of a mountain in Italy, the guy who wrote me a song called "Kayli Fever," the guy who all the best memories of my life were with. Deep down I knew we had to end things, but letting go of our romance was inconceivable.

Even though I felt like the dumpee rather than the dumper, I was the one to pull the plug. It was heartbreaking to abandon the dream of being together, but one of us had to do it. I guess it was both a blessing and a curse that we broke up while living in different countries. We could block out the other completely (with the exception of stupid fucking Facebook), but we never had any real sense of closure.

The last time we saw each other, the day I *hit* him, we sat on a bench and were brutally honest, telling of the new people we'd been seeing and how we'd been carrying on with our lives. He seemed to be doing better than I was. He had put real effort into working through our breakup, concentrating on his flourishing career and building up his emotional and financial strength. I, on the other hand, had spent a large amount of time avoiding my feelings, partying like a Hilton sister, traveling all over the place and dating several insignificant people for distraction. I was envious (and, let's face it, resentful) of his strength and progress. The anger I felt was not fair or mature, but it was how my pain manifested.

Now, three months later, I had a face and name to put to my nemesis. Oh, Jenna Jones, how could you?

Charlie and I gave it our best shot, but when it came down to it we wanted different things. The brave young lady in me wanted to accept it, but the immature brat just couldn't. There was nothing I could do, the sight of Jenna Jones made me want to pee, fart, vomit, and cry all at once. She was no longer an illusion, a fictional character he was making up. She was a real-life brunette and, based on my Google research, a stylist with an excellent résumé and a better ass than mine. That bitch.

# Cut the Shit

TWO MONTHS AFTER CHARLIE and I first broke up over Skype, I was having lunch with my friend Tom when I naively declared, "I'm over Charlie." It was done. I had accepted our breakup and moved on.

Tom laughed and said, "Maybe, but I doubt it. You're gonna feel it *all* over again when you find out he's moved on. When he's in a full-on relationship again, that's rock bottom."

Dammit, Tom. There was Jenna Jones with her arm around Charlie, smugly grinning at me on Facebook—and there I was eating a pint of ice cream at rock bottom.

I'll be honest; my comforter wasn't the only thing keeping me company after we split. I was always meeting men, but I hadn't met anyone who I had any connection with or a desire to commit to. Certainly no one who I would *publicize* on my Facebook status.

I got up and paced around my apartment. I needed someone to ground me, soothe me, and make me laugh at the ridiculous nature of my spaz attack. I could call my friends, but they'd all tell me the same thing: "She's a placeholder until he comes back to you." "You're soul mates, this is just a phase." Or, "Who needs him? He'll be sorry. You're the best thing that ever happened to him." And that I was hotter, cooler, smarter, more fun, and better in bed than Jenna Jones (which I obviously am!). That's what friends are for. They're liars and ego boosters.

I didn't want any more bullshit. I needed the truth, even if it was going to hurt. And there's only one place to go for that sort of pain—my granny. She has one setting: *real*. She's the only lady in my life with enough scandals and experiences under her belt to put me to shame. "I know how things take place and why they take place," she says, "because I've done it all."

The lady has been everywhere. I can't go anywhere, from the Caymans to Croatia, without hearing an anecdote about an adventure she had there or an opinion about the food. "Yugoslavia is actually very pretty, if you're into stray dogs and misery," she would say in her thick, nasally Jewish New Yorker accent. Or, "I've been to every goddamn island. They've been renamed three times since I've been there, but trust me, I know the Caribbean better than a pirate."

Granny is part Larry David, part Joan Rivers. She's not the sweet-talking, cookie-baking, crocheting type. She's a shit-talking, straight-shooting, adventure-seeking, gossipy yenta. About a decade ago she migrated from her New York City zip code to South Florida. Although the sunshine appeals to her, she can't stand the slower pace or the seniors who flock there. "They're all sitting around waiting to get shorter and die," she complains. Not Granny; she's itching to climb a mountain in Rwanda to see the gorillas. She insists on working five days a week, and the lady is as fashion forward as the celebs in *US Weekly*. Her wit, humor, and unending opinions never cease to entertain me. Friends are great at giving me the advice that

I want to hear, but Granny will tell me what I need to hear, and then some.

I called her down at her home in South Florida and dramatically recounted my Facebook revelation. "You dodged a bullet," she huffed. "If you'd stayed with him you'd be knocked up, fat, miserable, and married."

"But I love him!" I yelled. I was being a brat. I was *pretty* sure I wasn't in love with him anymore, but the sight of Jenna Jones was making me think, say, and do things I didn't mean.

"Bullshit, no you don't," she insisted. "It's been over a year. He was a nice guy but he never had his shit together. He's a beta, you need an alpha. Now he's this girl's problem." She paused. "You know, I told your mother you two would never work out."

"What? Why would you say that?"

"Because it was prominent that he was the follower and you were the leader in every way," she began. "Men can't handle that."

I moaned, partly in protest, partly in agreement.

"Are you sorry it happened?" she asked.

"No, of course not." I was slowly gaining back my sanity and perspective.

"Exactly," she said, "not sorry it happened. He was part of your growing up. Part of your life. Now it's time to *move on*."

# What's Love Got to Do with It?

I THREW MYSELF AN ONGOING pity party in the days, weeks, and months following our initial breakup. During this stage I called Granny repeatedly for support. I wasn't looking for empowering words, but rather I was in need of her sassy trash-talking rants. She turned my sweet ex into the biggest piece of shit. "He was too old for you. What is he, a pervert?" I laughed back tears. "Do you remember what he wore for Thanksgiving? He looked like that kid from *High School Musical*. Pants so low I could see his underpants!" In truth, he wore a perfectly nice plaid button-down shirt with a pair of tight-fitting jeans that at one moment accidentally gave a peek at the elastic band of his briefs, but I appreciated her critical version of his style.

"Why aren't you putting yourself out there more? Are you at least having *recreational* sex?" she asked. Oh, I had put myself out there.

Two weeks fresh into my singledom, I was a full-on mess at work. For my "uniform" in the club that night I wore a long chocolate-brown slip that was completely see-through on the left side. I was definitely not graceful or self-confident enough to pull it off, but after a few shots I almost didn't notice or care that my nipples were on display. *Some* might have described it as sophisticated, but in the spirit of Granny, we'll call a spade a spade. It was slutty. My coworker Jacki scoffed, "Oh Jesus, watch out. Is this single Kayli?"

"I am going to get laid tonight," I declared, trying my best to convince myself that it was what I wanted. I was still under Charlie's love spell and naively thought another man's penis could break it. The girls all nodded casually and offered encouraging words.

"Good, you look like a slut," Michelle said.

"The best way to get over someone is to get under someone else," Melissa winked.

"Wait, you haven't fucked anyone else yet? I thought you broke up two weeks ago?" Liz asked, baffled.

I looked down from the balcony where I was cocktailing. I was on the hunt for a prospective hookup. Bodies swayed, glasses clinked, music thumped—the club was alive. The clientele, an intoxicated mix of Euro-trash playboys, bankers, and models all grinded, giggled, and groped around me. The place reeked of sexuality. Charlie used to hate the idea of me in this environment.

I sauntered through the club, my heart hurting and hormones pounding. Reckless and desperate thoughts crawled through my mind. Every girl I had ever worked with at one time or another had gone home with someone she met there. I thought I could do it too. I tried shooting suggestive looks at a guy waiting in line for the bathroom; he interpreted my seduction as constipation.

I drank shots of tequila at the bar and chugged champagne at my tables while I looked around for the right prospect. Then I saw him:

Leaning casually against the bar, sipping a Peroni, was José, a sexy Argentinean scenester with a five-o'clock shadow and a slick leather jacket. He looked me up and down, then said, "Darling, you look incredibly beautiful tonight." Beautiful? Whorish? Either way, I'd take it. Within seconds I was shoving my tongue down his throat. I pretended to be someone else, someone with more prowess and sleaze than I was naturally capable of.

Here was my perfect rebound, a club rat who would be ready and willing to go to bed with me. He was a man who I would feel no connection with and he would feel no attachment to me. I thought it would be quick and easy; his dick would break Charlie's seal.

After spending the rest of the night ignoring my tables and making out with José in different locations around the club, my shift was coming to an end. "Wanna go grab some coffee and talk?" he asked.

I shook my head with unwavering determination. "No, I want you to take me home and fuck me."

He looked nervous. "Uh . . . what if I just wanted to cuddle and make out with you all night? Would that be all right?" he asked while delicately twirling a lock of my hair.

"No, I want to have *sex*," I said with the insistence of a seven-year-old brat demanding a ride on a pony. José gulped nervously, then protectively put his arm around my shoulders and led me out of the club.

I hopped onto his bicycle's handlebars, nipples and all, and he peddled me from the Lower East Side to his Tribeca studio. On the ten-minute ride I gave myself a pushy pep talk: *You're doing this. You are going to have sex with a stranger and this is your decision and you want this and this is the right thing and it's all perfect and great. This is happening. Just do it, you fucking sex goddess, you.*

Back at his place he introduced me to his pug, Mr. Hugo. I gave him an obligatory pet, then helped myself to a beer in his fridge. I took a large gulp, then jumped on top of José's lap and began tearing off his clothes. "Whoa, whoa," he said, pulling away from me. "Slow down."

I was on a mission; I could not decelerate. I stripped off my dress and ordered him to get a condom. He looked at me with an expression of both fear and confusion. Mr. Hugo barked wildly.

"Can't we just make out?" he asked.

"What? What's wrong with you?" I asked, growing more impatient with every passing second. "This shouldn't be an issue. Why won't you fuck me?" I was getting cruel, pathetic, and desperate, but I wouldn't relent.

He put his arm over my shoulders as he led me to the couch and sat me down. "Listen, babe, I've been trying to change the way I handle relationships and girls. I actually haven't slept with anyone in almost five months. I want sex to be something more special and less casual. You know what I mean?"

I had no idea what he meant. This was supposed to be my careless one-night stand and he was ruining it for me. He was being far too sensitive and caring. Who did he think he was? At *any* other point in my life I would have appreciated this, but not this night, not this sexual rendezvous.

I contemplated, looked around the room, glanced down at my naked body and his half-naked body, took a swig of my beer. I demanded again: "Get a condom."

Defeated, he nodded obediently and grabbed one out of a kitchen drawer. "All right, *fine*, let's do this."

We did it, as Mr. Hugo eagerly panted beside us. It was an even mix of horrible and hilarious. José made sounds I'd only ever heard before on Animal Planet. He bit his lip trying not to come since it had been so long, and I was biting mine trying to not to cry. I missed Charlie. As soon as it was over I grabbed my clothes and tried to bolt. Isn't that what the loose ladies in the movies do?

"Darling, come on. Spend the night, lie down," he insisted. I huffed but agreed. It was the least I could do after he complied with my mission.

I laid back down and looked at the clouds painted above his bed. "Nice clouds," I said sarcastically. *Then* he started to explain the feng shui in his apartment and, even further, his beliefs in reincarnation and his past life as a warrior peasant who slayed a king. At this point I was ready to run, but I knew I'd have to wait for him to pass out (or slay him).

As the sun came up, he grabbed my arm and pulled it over him. He made *me* spoon *him*—I was big spoon and he was little spoon—a maneuver one should *never* contort to on a one-night stand. I cringed and frowned against his back. Mr. Hugo cuddled up against me. As soon as I was sure he was asleep, I wiggled out of the dog sandwich, grabbed my stuff, and ran.

And shocker, I was wrong; a stranger's dong was not the cure for my Charlie addiction, but that doesn't mean I stopped experimenting with this technique. When you're brokenhearted you'll try anything to move forward. However, sleeping around with losers is a slippery slope. In my post-breakup year, through a series of sexual escapades that never evolved into anything further than the experience itself, I learned how easy it is to stay chronically single in New York. In this city lovers can become strangers faster than your MetroCard runs out.

So, to answer Granny's question: "Are you at least having *recreational* sex?"

Yes, I *had* been having recreational sex, but that's exactly what it was, and in general it was shit. "Oh God, we're not talking about this. I just haven't met anyone recently that I feel like I could love," I admitted.

"How does that song go?" Granny asked. "You know, 'what's love got to do, got to do with it?'"

She was quoting Tina Turner to express her opinion about my sex life.

# An Affair to Remember

G RANNY WAS FAILING to comprehend the sea of regret that I was swimming in. My ship had sunk and I was alone on a pathetic island of self-pity. And *he* had Jenna Jones. I felt like I lost the best thing that ever happened to me and now this English twat had him. I went to Granny with my biggest fear: "What if I never meet anyone I feel that way about again?"

This was a question I was plagued with. I had been hitting Granny with it on a weekly basis since the day I decided not to follow Charlie to London. When you fall in love for the first time it feels like the most unique experience, like you're the only two people in the world who have ever discovered this drug and no one else would ever get it or be able to re-create it.

After dealing with countless hysterical phone calls in the months following my breakup, about how Charlie was "the one" and how could I ever meet anyone who would compare, I wore Granny down. I opened an old wound and brought memories to the surface that she had thought were long buried.

Days after my Jenna Jones breakdown she called me. "I need to tell you something."

"Lay it on me," I demanded.

She huffed, she hemmed, she paused, she tried to change the subject. Then, finally, with a stern tone she spoke. "I called him."

I had no idea who "him" was.

"Ira," she whispered.

I thought for a moment but couldn't recall the name. "Who is that?"

She practically screamed through the receiver. "The affair, goddammit!"


Throughout my youth I often commented on Granny's Cartier watches or jewels, asking, "Where did you get that?"

She'd always give the same nonchalant response: "An admirer."

Or I would be traveling somewhere like Perugia, Italy, and she'd tell me a place to eat. When questioned about her trips she'd just say, "I went with a friend." Very cryptic, very Granny.

When I was in film school I tried making a documentary about monogamy and chose Granny as one of my first interviewees. She alluded to stepping outside of her marriage, but I was naive and probably too self-involved to dig deeper (no surprise, I never made it as a documentary filmmaker). In the process of shooting I developed a sour view on the subject of marriage and thought it better to call it quits before I became a twenty-one-year-old with the romantic optimism of a middle-aged divorcée.

Had I not been so self-centered I would have learned back

then that Ira and Granny had an affair that ran longer than her marriage. It persisted even after her divorce, carrying on for a total of thirty-two years. Somewhere in the shuffle of my own life and heartbreak, I neglected to learn about Granny's.

It had been decades since they spoke and almost *thirty years* since they ended their relationship. He was the love of her life, her love drug, the man she ended her marriage for, the one who no one measured up to. It was the romance that she had never moved past.

As hard as her exterior can be—and trust me, it is hard—Granny is still human. She has lived, loved, hurt, healed, and evolved. I always thought that she was alone because she was old and that was her choice. When people look at their grandparents they usually don't think about the reality of their relationships and heartbreaks or their youthful scandals. They think of sciatica and baked goods.

When I look at Granny I think of a woman who has been through it all. She was only nineteen when she got married and had my mother; even back in her day it was a young age to commit. She wasn't ready for any of it, but she saw it as her only option.

At sixteen, her mother passed away from cancer. "Oh, I was a wild child in those days," she bragged. "Three dates in one night was no big thing." Even I was impressed with that kind of stamina. "I had no supervision, no one saying, 'Where are you going for dinner?' What do you think girls on their own did?"

After her mother died, her father refused to play the role of single dad to a teenage daughter. He took off for Chicago and she was left to fend for herself in Forest Hills, Queens, New York. Her friends' mothers would occasionally insist on her coming over for a meal, but for the most part she was on her own.

When she was seventeen there were three main men on her dance card: Joe the sweetheart, John the wealthy teenager, and Lenny the gangster. Joe was twice her age and drove a fancy Cadillac. "He had a face that only a mother could love," she said. "But he was a nice man, no denying that. He never laid a finger on me."

He used to call her and say, "What are you doing for dinner tomorrow night, kid?" Without a real home or mother, she never knew. "Why don't you know where you're eating? I know what you're gonna do. You're gonna have dinner with me." He was good to her but there was no sizzle. Why is it that the ones who treat us the best are rarely the ones we want?

It was John who she was swooning for. Young teenage love, he probably would have been the best match for her out of all of them. He came from a well-off family that wanted to see their boy go off to a fancy university, become a doctor, and marry a nice lady from a good family. A Jewish girl from Queens without any parents or social status would not do it for their boy. In order to ensure their son would do right by them, his parents bought him a car and paid his tuition fees at Stanford University. He drove away and never looked back.

Once John was out of the picture she was left with Lenny, an older man, with a wife and kids, and a tendency to gamble and lie. "He was fun though. Of course dating a gangster is always fun," she told me.

The fun ended when she got pregnant. Still in high school, without a family support system, she didn't know what to do. Lenny took her to a broken-down tenement and told her they'd live there together; he'd split his time between his family and her. His offer was less than appealing. "I was no dummy," she told me. "I knew a bad deck of cards when I was dealt one. My life would be over before it even began."

This was 1954, and abortion was illegal. Clearly that wouldn't deter Granny. I picture her like Penny in *Dirty Dancing* (minus the tango moves): broke, scared, and desperate. With a big wad of cash from Lenny in her pocket, she went to an under-the-table doctor to perform the procedure.

"I was heartbroken. I had messed up, big-time, but I couldn't live that kind of life," she confessed to me almost sixty years after the incident. But it was over with Lenny and she wanted to move forward, so she enrolled at New York University and tried to take control of her life.

Without the financial support from the gangster, she was back to fending for herself. She took a job as a receptionist and held a part-time gig as a shoe model to pay the bills. "If I had been a half a size smaller I would have made it big in Spain. Those Spanish love a small foot," she recalled.

She was struggling to make ends meet when she met my grandfather Mark at the Vanderbilt Hotel. She found him to be charming and agreeable enough to go steady with. "I was going downhill fast and hard. I knew I needed to make a move if I was going to survive so I went eeny, meeny, miny, mo and chose him." She was still a teenager, yet she was already willing to settle in order to change her life and put the past behind her.

After a few weeks of dating, Mark was heading to the Catskills for the summer with some friends. "That's when I cried my famous tear," she bragged. He asked her why she looked so sad, and she told him she didn't want to see him go.

"So marry me?" he suggested. And she did. She didn't

want to be on her own anymore, yet she was too inexperienced to understand what she was compromising by becoming a wife to someone she barely knew at such a young age.

Things took a turn three short years later. She was at dinner with her husband and another couple, the man of which was Mark's boss, Ira. Ira locked eyes with Granny throughout the meal and later pursued her relentlessly. After a few months of sneaky dinners and hushed phone calls, the two were fully involved in a smoking-hot affair.

"It was a very volatile relationship; it was never solid because it was crazy. When things are crazy they're exciting," she told me. "We'd have terrible fights, say terrible things to each other, then he'd call and say, 'Honey, how are you?' I'd say, 'Did I hear you right? What's your name?' Then he'd say, 'Darling, I got us two tickets to London.'"

She did all sorts of devious things to cover her tracks. She created a make-believe friend that she would tell her husband she was traveling with; Ira even went so far as to send a girl over to play the role of the "gal pal" so Mark would buy the story. She pretended to have a job as a salesperson to explain how she was managing to finance her travel.

"Where would you go when you lied and told your husband you were at work?" I asked.

"My part-time job was Ira."

After sneaking around for more than twenty-five years, the two of them decided to give their love a real shot. They separated from their spouses and moved in together, but now they were both middle-aged people in a real life setting. They went from romantic nights at the Ritz to reality in Ridgewood, New Jersey. No more jet-setting or fancy dinners, or the thrilling butterflies that come when engaging in romantically shameful deeds. Suddenly they were no longer *lovers*, they were domestic partners. After only a few months Ira went back to his wife and Granny divorced her husband, remaining single to this day.

Granny saw my fear and heartache and they awakened within her the love story of her own life. Ira was her Charlie. The feelings were still there. So she called him. After more than thirty years he still had the same home number. When he heard her voice through the receiver he asked, "Is this the little lady that got away from me?" His vocal cords were shakier than she remembered, but it was still him.

My heart broke for Granny and Ira. The two of them sat on the phone crying about how they were the love of each other's life and the regret they carried for not trying harder to make it work, for not recognizing the rarity in their spark. But of course now it was too late; Ira was eighty-eight, still married to the same woman, and Granny had grown used to her independent way of life.

What a pathetic pair. Granny and me, living in the past, fearing the future, and being overall bitter bitches. We were wasting time wallowing on the sidelines. We had to face the fact that neither of us was getting any younger or doing anything productive for our love lives.

Granny kept trying to drill in my head: "How you gonna know that vanilla's your favorite flavor if you haven't tried the rest of the lot?" She didn't want me out sampling *all* thirty-two varieties, but she wanted me to be open to a little mint chip or mocha in the mix, to not waste time on regrets or the past. I knew I needed to get moving with my romantic life again, but the dating world was foreign to me.

The problem was not meeting men. Working in a high-end nightclub doing bottle service for half a decade, I was always *meeting* men, just not the right ones. Men who met me in that environment had a much dirtier definition of the word "date" than I was up for. The job description walks a fine line between waitress and stripper. I served alcohol and kept my clothes on, and there was never any funny business, but the male attention could be just as lewd and repulsive.

Granny had been encouraging me to play the field for months. "You're twenty-four, you're never gonna be as young as you are today. You think the options will be so plentiful in ten years?" Granny has always wanted the best for me, urging me to enjoy every opportunity that comes my way. In her opinion the best route is the one most traveled. More men, more experiences, more life.

I needed to wipe Charlie off my mind and find a way to meet men, all types of men who had no connection to nightlife or any of my other social circles. Where were all the good guys? I had no clue where to find them or how to seduce them.

How would I know what I even wanted in a man if I never dated around to begin with? If you're buying a car and being responsible about it, you don't just buy the first car you see; you look around, do your research, maybe even take a few for a spin. You figure out which features are important to you and the ones you can do without. She wanted me to try everything from the used Camry to the shiny Camaro.

# The Favorite Granddaughter

"**Y**OU KNOW YOUR SISTER'S moving in with her boyfriend?" Granny called to inform me. "You know she met him on one of those dating websites?" This was not a subtle hint.

My older sister, Danielle, is the model granddaughter. Since as far back as I can remember, Granny has shamelessly referred to her as "the favorite granddaughter." Although she claims it's *mainly* for comedic purposes, I know there's a shred of truth in her title. She was the first born, the good girl, who did the best in school and never got a drunk tattoo of her friend's initials on her left butt cheek. My sister's hunk of a boyfriend was clearly scoring her some solid points in Granny's book.

"Are you trying to suggest something?" I asked. Online dating? Who did she think I was? I am a young social butterfly with a perky pair of 34Ds. I met Charlie on the street outside my apartment in New York City. Our relationship was impulsive, passionate, and the furthest thing from building an online dating profile.

"Cool your jets and lose the tone, kid," she warned. "It wouldn't be a bad idea for you to get out there and mix it up."

I wasn't about to cave. "What about you? Why don't *you* online date? You should *mix it up*."

Earlier that summer Granny had called to tell me about a date she had been set up on with an eighty-plus senior. It was supposed to be her stab at forgetting Ira (*again*), but it was a disaster. First her date asked if she would meet him at the restaurant so he could save money on gas. Then he set the date for 5 p.m. so they could make the early-bird special (Granny is not an early-bird kind of bird). Over fondue, the shriveled-up cheapskate seductively licked cheese off a square of sourdough bread as he confessed, "I'm a very talented kisser." For once, Granny was speechless. "I just thought you should know because kissing is about the only way for me to express my desire these days."

She and I got a good laugh out of it, but it definitely didn't do anything positive in the way of getting her out on the single scene. To make matters worse, after that first tearful call to Ira, their relationship sparked back up. With her in Florida and him still in New York (and still very much married), the two began a telephone affair. Their chats were like a roller coaster. She'd call me after a heated argument to vent: "He's still the same self-involved bastard he was fifty years ago." Then days later she'd call back giggling about something sweet he said. A charming man is a dangerous entity.

Their relationship was inappropriate on a lot of levels. Although the hopeless romantic in me rooted for them and their timeless love, the realist in me knew it couldn't last and understood how wrong their phone calls really were.

It wasn't my place to intervene, and luckily I didn't have to. One day Granny called and said, "It's over. He broke my heart. *Again*."

My heart broke for hers. "What happened?"

"He got old. His problems are old. Our issues are old. No use in hashing them out anymore. It's done. We are done."

After thirty years there was finally a closed door. It was a huge relief, a weight off her tiny shoulders. The loving granddaughter in me wanted her to date again to get back her mojo and have a second lease on life. The selfish granddaughter in me wanted her to start dating again so I could hear more hilarious stories about cranky old men and impotence.

Mutual bullying ensued. We both rattled off reasons why we thought the other should be online dating. Oddly both of us held up a similar case: You're too entertaining to be alone. You need to see what else is out there. You're out of practice, you don't remember how to date. It could be fun!

Besides Granny's irrational fear of having her identity stolen, our arguments against online dating were also the same: What if someone we know sees us on these sites? The men on them are all losers. Our egos were too big. And when it came down to it, we were both stuck on the serendipity of finding romance in real life.

The argument to online date was more convincing when I thought of my sister and her boyfriend and their perfect relationship. Everyone who meets them can't help but remark on how well suited they are. They're a cyber novelty, but they did give the sites more credibility in Granny's and my eyes. We tried our best to get on board with the concept that how you meet someone is just the prologue; the real meat is in the chapters.

Match.com advertises that one out of five relationships begins online. That's a pretty compelling statistic. The romantic fantasy of spotting your soul mate while perusing the aisles of a quaint bookstore is totally outdated. Who goes to a store when you have the web? The Internet is the key to everything these days—we shop for books, music, clothes, and, increasingly, companionship online.

With some serious coaxing on both ends, we came to terms with the idea and decided to follow the favorite granddaughter's lead. It's an experiment, we told each other, as a way to ease ourselves back into the dating game.

Through an oral agreement, we committed to our dating journey for twelve months. Over the course of the year we'd sharpen our dating skills while sampling the thirty-two flavors. It was time to relinquish our egos, bury the stigma, and embrace the humility of the online dating process.

# 75 Yr Old Woman
# Seeks 75 Yr Old Man

"**G**IVE ME A FAKE NAME. I like Deborah," Granny said. Since she lives in South Florida and I'm in New York, we made her JDate profile together over the phone.

"Deborah?"

"I want to make an alter ego, you know, a fake personality?"

"That doesn't make any sense," I told her. "You would be incapable of maintaining a fake personality through a whole date."

"I'm the most deceptive person you know"—she cackled like a ruthless kingpin—"I lie to you all the time and you don't know it."

I wondered if this devious minx was even really my granny.

After an agonizing hour of encouragement she began to get into it. Body type? I suggested we put down petite, she preferred adding shapely or voluptuous. The ultimate deceiver insisted we significantly decrease her age. For an older lady, she's a hot commodity, but I still thought it would be best to stick with the truth. "They're all doin' it, trust me," she insisted. "And I betcha they all put down that they listen to jazz. They think it makes 'em sound young and hip. Like, 'Look at me, I listen to the horn!'" I don't know any hip dudes who get down with the horn, but I wasn't about to argue with her.

She is barely over five feet, but like me she wanted a taller man. "He better be at least five-eight. I don't want any fashrimpadickas like your mother's dating." ("Fashrimpadicka" is one of Granny's fake Yiddish words that she uses to describe short, creepy men.)

I started checking boxes to hone in on her type. "Would you say you'd like a worldly man?"

"Wealthy? Definitely," she said.

"No, no, 'worldly,'" I corrected.

She laughed. "I like wealthy. Yes, definitely put down wealthy. Worldly isn't bad either though."

When we started off she insisted on keeping her "About Me" and "What I'm Looking For" sections vague. She was hesitant to reveal too much. "Less is more, less is more," she assured me. When you're defining yourself online, it can feel easier to lie, or dance around the truth, rather than admit who you are. I don't recommend it, but I understand it.

Then it was my turn. I chose OkCupid because the word on the street was that it had the best-looking fellas. It's the site my sister met her boyfriend on and was recommended to me by a few friends who were willing to *admit* to online dating. OkCupid is also free, the perfect price for my cheap ass.

I struggled with choosing a username that would come across as carefree *and* seductive. It's almost impossible not to come off cheesy in a screen name. I'm ashamed to admit that I even googled ideas. DolphinLover62, Bonerz4U, NYCbabez13, and gr8nbed were some names I came across.

Then there was the humbling step of choosing a picture. Oh God, the pictures. "Nothing slutty, but something appealing, you know, friendly," Granny advised.

Although most people had several pictures up, I started with one. Subtle and sexy. My sister suggested having a photo that was shoulders up. "You get more clicks if it's just your head," she advised. I went with a shot from a barbecue two summers ago. I looked tan, approachable, and probably a couple of points hotter than I do in real life. As soon as the picture uploaded, I felt the same doubts that Granny had. Suddenly my face was out there on the Internet for all exes, acquaintances, friends, and strangers to see.

"Let's fill the rest of my info out later," I suggested.

I hung up and went to the gym. The weight machines were packed with men between the ages of twenty-four and thirty-eight, the same age range I was under on OkCupid. *Shit*, I thought, *someone in here might recognize me!* I hung my head low on the elliptical, trying to sweat away my anxiety.

After showering I logged back on to find twenty-seven new messages from possible suitors. I still hadn't uploaded any info, so the messages I got were based on my "friendly" picture and the fact that I had accidentally checked the box that said I was into "casual sex."

I had messages from Staten Island guidos, World of Warcraft enthusiasts, and everything in between:

"Wanna cuddle?"

"I'm an Asian doctor. Interested?"

"Yo buttaface, I got girlz hotter than u."

"Beautiful hair. Are those natural curls?"

"Hi sweety u wanna have sexy time?"

"Hi, I am a 42 year old Spanish man, 5'9 tall, 180 lbs with a fit body, black hair, brown eyes and looking for a friendship for a casual affair."

The messages I was receiving ranged from creepy (yet weirdly flattering) to downright offensive. I was intimidated but decided that adding more information might help with the process of elimination and weeding out the casual-sex-searching monkeys.

Suddenly I had to decide: Am I stylish? How about spontaneous? Kind? Do I want to have kids? Do I care if my partner smokes? Do I expect a phone call from my partner every day? Multiple times a day? Ugh. Alone, I sat at my computer, sweating and moaning out loud from the pangs of embarrassment.

I called Granny. A word of advice: When creating a profile it's a good idea to have someone help you fill in the blanks. It can be intimidating and totally overwhelming to do on your own. Granny bullied me the same way I did to her and I whined the same way she did to me. We argued over what parts of my life were important to reveal.

Besides selling overpriced booze to wealthy snobs, I also started a charity in Kenya for education. The organization buys textbooks and awards college scholarships to orphaned schoolchildren in Nairobi. My work in Kenya is beyond fulfilling and helps to justify prancing around in stilettos to pay the bills. I spend two months out of the year in Kenya, which provides a bizarre balance between both jobs. They're two conflicting worlds that were hard and, I thought, unnecessary to articulate on OkCupid.

"Don't put anything about your nightlife gig, they'll get the wrong idea," Granny insisted, and then continued to preach to me for the millionth time about why I should stop working as a bottle server. "You know you're never gonna meet a nice man that's comfortable with you shaking your tush in a little dress and slinging alcohol to snot-faced millionaires," she warned. "You should put down that you're charitable, you're a philanthropist, you're well traveled. Put, 'I hope I'm fun. I think I am.'"

I decided to go with her "less is more" motto.

"How about age range? How old do you think is *too* old for me?" I asked.

"I don't know. Double your age, I guess," she suggested.

"What? That's obscene." I cracked up. "You would freak out if I brought home a forty-eight-year-old."

She agreed. "Okay, okay. Only double your age if you're just fooling around. If you're getting serious, no one over ten years older than you." I tried to picture her reaction if I admitted to hooking up with a forty-eight-year-old man. I imagined lots of judgmental lip pursing.

The process was just heating up and we were already having fun. My sister gave me some advice: "There are some hilarious, repulsive, and questionable moments that go down in online dating; it's best to have a partner in crime."

I couldn't think of a better wingman than Granny. She'd been through it all, and now I had her as my pal and punching bag in this process.

# I Don't Make Dinner,
# I Make Reservations

IF WE MET MEN online who could change our lives, spark our attractions, make us fall head over heels, give us (me . . . I think the window has closed for Granny) the urge to make babies and wed—that would be incredible. But it wasn't our goal. We wanted to *date*, something that I missed out on in my formative college years and Granny hadn't given a shot in decades. I wanted to learn about myself and the kind of man I wanted to be with. We both needed to open up to the idea of romance again. Neither of us was willing to admit that we had hopes of finding a real match. What was more important was to learn about who we were—our tastes, tics, and talents.

We'd literally and digitally put ourselves out there and now it was time to get into it. After fiddling around on the sites for a few weeks, dabbling with an addiction to reading all the flirty messages we were receiving, we had to let go of being gun-shy, get off the sidelines, and give it a real go. I called Granny and announced that it was game time.

I logged on to Granny's JDate profile. Although she is

far from a practicing Jew, she is Jew-ish and has spent most of her romantic life with Jews, and she loves pastrami on rye and making up words that sound like Yiddish but in fact are not. I thought it best to keep her in a good comfort zone. We started sifting through her suitors.

"You're really stressing me out, kid. Read me their profiles. I'm going to relax on my terrace."

Granny is basically computer illiterate, so I scrolled through her admirers for her. It was a good deal for both of us. She could sit back in her lounge chair while spying for call girls on Tiger Woods's boat from her terrace, and I got to giggle at the profiles of old men filled with glamour shots and affinities for backgammon and grandchildren.

After I heard her exhale and take a swig of Merlot, I was confident Granny was in her most relaxed position. "This guy is seventy-four, from New York, has three kids, loves golf and going to the movies, he's a Taurus—" I began before she cut me off.

"Taurus? No way. Taurus and Sagittarius—not a good match," she said.

"What? Since when do you follow horoscopes? What do you even know about star signs?" I asked.

"Oy, trust me. A friend told me. Or maybe it was Pisces and Sagittarius? Either way, let's hear another."

"Okay, this guy is eighty—" I started again.

"Eighty? No way. How am I gonna go on a date with an eighty-year-old? He's probably blind, halfway dead, and in need of nurse, not a date."

Granny was seventy-five, definitely a sprightly seventy-five, but like many people, Granny sees herself as younger than she is. Bodies may change but heads and hearts do not.

I continued going through the list as she shot down one after another. "Big eater? He must be a real heifer," "Never married? Psychopath," "Likes to salsa dance? Yeah right, he's seventy-eight, I bet he can barely walk."

As cringe-worthy as it felt for me to be online dating, I knew I needed to be more sensitive to Granny. The process was so foreign to any romantic experience that she was familiar with. Facebook (or, as Granny refers to it, "that book with all the faces") is only a step away from scoping out people to date on the web. For Granny this was an alien way of interacting.

"Let's do yours. I wanna hear what all the schmaltzy schmucks have to say to you," she said.

I read her one from a thirty-two-year-old music producer who loves "a home-cooked meal." She cackled. "You couldn't cook if your life depended on it. Write back, 'I don't make dinner, I make reservations.'"

She was right, besides, he wasn't appealing enough for a face-to-face interaction. I read another from an Irish guy who was new to New York. "Irish? Oh no, you can't date him. He's a big drinker, probably an alcoholic. You know, the Irish have that drinking gene."

I clicked on a photo of a handsome man. "He's from Chicago, family and friends are important to him, likes playing basketball, he was a marine—"

"Well, he's not Jewish then," she cut me off.

"First off, how would you know that? Second off, why does that matter?" I asked.

"It doesn't matter, I'm just sayin' what Jewish marines do you know?"

I actually didn't know any marines either way, nor did I care if a guy was Jewish. The number of penises I have seen would terrify Granny, not because of the quantity but rather for the percentage that were uncircumcised.

There was one message from a sexy bearded man that jumped out at me. "Ahem . . . I've rated you 4 stars . . . added you to my favorites . . . and winked . . . I've run out of passive-aggressive ways of getting your attention . . . :/ I live in Williamsburg, I make videos all day, my mom thinks I'm cute. Robert."

Granny said it was smart of him to rate me only four out of five stars. "He's got you just where he wants you. Now you want to be rated five stars, right? He wants you to work for it."

Who doesn't want some validation? It's like the men's pickup book *The Game* by Neil Strauss, where he trains men to "neg" women. "Negging" is defined as "a light insult wrapped in the package of a compliment." This felt like a neg to me, and unfortunately I am an easy target for a backhanded compliment. Granny was right, I did want to be rated five stars, dammit.

I clicked through his profile. There were pictures of him leaning against his single-speed bicycle in the park, relaxing with friends in a coffee shop (I think I saw a book by Milan Kundera, my favorite author, resting on his lap) — there was even one of him holding a baby. Men with babies are my lady-porn kryptonite. (Disclaimer: I don't want a baby at this point in time, but that will not stop me from drooling over a man with a child in his arms.)

In my head I let myself build him up into a funny, intelligent, kombucha-brewing Williamsburg hipster. I liked this guy. He was going to make me laugh, send me funny website links, take me to cool underground shows, bike with me on the weekends, and probably convince me to get matching tattoos on some wild night out that we'd laugh about for years as we recounted the story to friends.

I messaged him back: "I'm blushing from all of your cyber flirts. Fine, I'm hooked. Let's get a drink?" I don't know why it didn't occur to me to engage in more conversation before jumping into suggesting an alcoholic beverage. I was a newbie; I didn't know how the game worked.

"Your profile is very sparse," he replied. "Wait, the only photo of you is one where you are holding a drink. Now, early in the morning at 9:30 a.m., you suggest getting a drink . . . should I be worried? Is an intervention too intense for a first date? But yes, a drink. When?"

I blushed at my computer screen. I did have only one picture, but so what? It was a good one. I was tan and happy at a barbecue. I love summer, hot dogs, and outdoor drinking. It exuded everything I felt I wanted to express.

I wrote back: "Busted! Big lush over here. Too drunk to fill out more on my profile. Let's meet tonight?" I chose Ten Bells, a bar in my neighborhood, to meet up. It seemed like a good option because: a) I'm lazy and it's only a few blocks from my apartment; b) I rarely go there, so the chances of bumping into friends who might throw me off my game were slim; c) the dim lighting they implement is most flattering with my skin tone; and d) they sell oysters, and I thought some aphrodisiacs might come in handy.

And so it was settled. I was going to have my very first online date. Then the nerves sunk in. How would we recognize each other? What would I wear? Who would pay for the drinks? What if he's a psycho-rapist-murderer who wants to wear my skin like a robe to the opera?

It had been ages since I had a formal date. Does my generation even do that anymore? Would a shared bagel from the deli after a regrettable night count? I called Granny in a fit of anxiety. As I talked a mile a minute, she silently listened and quietly judged, until piping up, "If he's not a stud, you're in New York City. Maybe the guy on the barstool next to you will be even cuter." A lady on the prowl, you have to admire that.

Granny plotted with me like a teenage girl. "If he's a creep, call me then hang up. I'll call back and say I'm dying." A dying grandma would be an excellent excuse to flee. I hoped it wouldn't come to that but I did appreciate the offer.

# Players Gonna Play

WHILE GETTING DRESSED for my date, I chose the most complimentary summer dress in my closet—tons of cleavage, lots of leg, and a flashy coral color. I was going to wow this man. I rode my bike to the bar and strutted down Broome Street ready to fall head over heels. In my head Destiny's Child was singing an anthem for me. Oh no, Robert was not ready for my jelly.

My booming confidence disappeared as soon as I opened the doors to the crowded bar and reality sunk in. I was about to have an online date. There are few experiences in my life that have brought on such an extreme case of nerves—it's right up there with a big interview or giving your first blow job.

Would people around me know that I had sunk to the Internet for romance? How was I going to recognize Robert in the sea of men with beards, and why were they all wearing identical checkered shirts?

I took a deep breath and squeezed through the thin corridor to find a seat at the bar. Suddenly I was brutally aware of the obscene amount of cleavage I was revealing. Perhaps I went too far with the dress. As I stared down at my bare skin,

I tried to estimate how many millimeters away from a nipple slip I was when I felt a tap on my shoulder. I looked up and saw Robert, or at least a man who most closely resembled the pictures I had seen of Robert. He was also staring at my boobs, which were at his eye level.

"Kayli?" he asked, his lips forming a wry smile. I was sitting on a stool that added an extra inch to my five-foot-seven height, and yet I was looking down at Robert. His profile had listed him at five-eleven but this man was no taller than five-eight. I know it's shallow, but I like tall men. I need a guy who can tower over me so that I feel small in comparison. If I'm straddling a skinny man (yes, this is what goes through my head), or walking down the street with my arm around the waist of a man who is shorter than me, I'm going to have body issues, plain and simple. My confidence can't handle the blow of a small man. This guy was definitely smaller than me, and what made it more annoying was he had falsely advertised in his profile.

In my state of surprise and confusion, I went in for an aggressive double-cheek kiss/hug/handshake. My awkward greeting shut both of us up for a moment, until he took his seat beside me and bashfully handed me two lottery tickets as an introductory present.

I looked at the tickets. "For me?" I asked with such hesitation you would have thought English was my second language. He nodded. It was a cute yet risky idea to give a lottery ticket to kick off a date. If I had won, it would have been an auspicious start, but I lost.

"This is my first online date," I blurted out.

He nodded like he already knew. "Yeah, I thought something was up from your profile and messages."

"Why? What was wrong with them?" I asked defensively.

"Well, it was just weird that you had barely any info and then suggested getting a drink without more back and forth. Typically people friend each other on Facebook to get more of a feel for the person, but yeah, you kind of went shotgun style."

I'm not really a fan of Facebook, especially after it led me to Jenna Jones. Facebook turns me into a psycho stalker, and I'm sketchy enough without it. Besides, friending an OkCupider and giving him access to all my revealing pictures and info about my friends so he can see who we might know in common felt unnecessary.

Through real-life chatting rather then Internet lurking, I learned that Robert was from the Midwest and worked in production design for film shoots. He didn't like to read (I scratched the possible Milan Kundera connection off our list of similarities). The bike he was standing next to in his profile picture belonged to his roommate; in fact, he was terrified of biking in the city. He had no tattoos and no plans to get any. By this point I decided it was safe to assume he did not brew his own kombucha.

When it was my turn, I came off equal parts conceited and self-deprecating. I explained my work, the trips I had taken over the summer, and somehow let it slip that I was try-ing to get over an ex.

He pulled at his collar. I went too far. "You talk a lot," he said. I blushed. I couldn't shut my goddamn mouth. Any nor-mal person knows not to bring up their ex on a first (or sec-ond or third . . .) date, but my nerves got the better of me.

He took out his phone and opened the OkCupid app. "Let's see if we're compatible," he suggested. When you enroll on OkCupid, you have to answer several compatibility questions to see if you're a "match." This felt like an odd activity but I went with it.

We differed on almost every question until I cut him off. This was unnecessary; we didn't need a phone app to tell us what was apparent in reality: we were incompatible. While exiting the list he accidentally clicked on his messages, which revealed his large cache of OkCupid women and their Internet interactions. By the looks of it, online dating was Robert's part-time job. The twinkle of pride I felt from his online winks, star rating, and messages was fading fast. Robert was not the adorable hipster I built him up to be.

He switched gears with his phone and went into his photos to show me a fish he had caught over the weekend, his nephew, and a sunset from Morocco. It was clear he wanted me to be impressed, so I suggested we just switch phones, flip through them, and get a feel for each other's lives.

In Robert's phone I found many recent pictures of a pretty girl in bed and far too many pictures of cats. He owned three (cats, not girls). Terrific.

While he went through my phone, I saw his eyes light up with confusion, excitement, and wonder. My friends are attractive and we take silly pictures in fun places. He got far back into my photos, about two years back, when he stumbled on the picture that I had for my OkCupid profile.

"You can't have a pic of you from two years ago—that's cheating," he informed me.

I was twenty-four not forty-six. I didn't think it was a big deal but Robert wouldn't let it go. "You need to put more photos of you and things that you like to do," he suggested. "Like travel ones or silly ones, maybe some arty sepia-toned ones, you know?"

I didn't agree. I took my phone back and declared the game over. The phone swap is an accelerated way of getting to know someone. It's better than Facebook because you don't just see what the other person wants you to see; instead you get a full-on view of his or her day-to-day life. I wouldn't recommend this activity for the bashful — or if you think there's even a slight chance you might be interested in dating the person you're playing with.

Although I already knew Robert was a dating junkie and therefore not for me, I didn't know how to hop off the date train. When he suggested moving to another spot on the block, I shook my head "no," but annoyingly the word my mouth formed was "yes."

We went next door to Barrio Chino, a Mexican restaurant I loved for its margaritas. I ordered my favorite, a jalapeno-infused fireball. Unaware of how spicy the drink was, Robert followed my lead. It was painful watching him pretend to enjoy the drink as sweat beaded on his forehead.

"So it sounds like you know a lot about OkCupid," I said.

He then whipped out his trusty iPhone *again* and opened the app once more. "Do you know about the broadcast option?" The terrified look in my eyes gave him my answer. "You can post your location and see other people who are in close proximity to you."

"Like the app where you can see all the sexual predators near your location?" I asked, joking.

"Exactly," he said, not joking. He loaded it and the faces of some sassy ladies appeared.

To experiment, we broadcasted that he was on an OkCupid date that was going terribly wrong and he needed someone to come save him. As he sat perusing his phone, mine rang. It was Granny. I politely excused myself and went outside to answer it. Before I could even say hello—

"Listen to this bullshit," she demanded. "This man emails me on JDate, *very* flirty, tells me he's going to call me tonight, and guess what?" She paused for emphasis. "*Nothing*, absolutely nothing!"

"Granny, maybe you missed the call, or maybe he's going to call tomorrow. But listen, I have to go, I'm still on the date," I reminded her.

"Oh, hubba hubba! How's it going? Is he cute? It's pretty late, how long you gonna schlep this thing on for?"

"He's nice, but short." I rushed her off the phone and promised I'd call in the morning. Just as I hung up the phone rang again.

"Sorry, just needed to tell you, he did call, that bastard did call! I just saw that I had missed it on the caller ID. Have fun with the fashrimpadicka," she hung up.

Meanwhile, back at the bar Robert sat trying to look smooth while sucking on ice cubes to cool his tongue from the spicy beverage. There were still no bites on the broadcast.

Granny was right, it was getting late and I had no desire to learn any more about this man, his cats, or his OkCupid expertise.

Robert walked me to my bicycle, which was chained up to a street sign. He seductively leaned against the post trying his best to summon some James Dean suave. "Give me your number," he insisted. I hesitated, I didn't really want this phone addict to have my digits, but in a weak moment I caved and forked it over. "Can I friend you on Facebook?" he asked.

"No thank you," I said politely, as if declining a piece of a cookie.

As I mounted my bike he took a step forward to plant a kiss on me. We did a dance of the heads, he moved toward me and I shifted left, then right, then left, then up, then down. Before he had the chance to lay one on me, I pushed on my pedal and rode forward into the night. It was an asshole move on my part, but I wasn't sure if I was the kind of gal who kisses on her first Internet date.

"You are *definitely* a girl who kisses on the first date," Granny said. "You just weren't into him." I expected Granny to be confused by all the technology references when I recounted my story, but the real shock for her came from Robert's choice of pets.

"Cats? Three? A man? Disgusting," she said.

I agreed.

"Well, you weren't going to marry him."

I definitely was not going to marry him. It was a bummer that I let myself imagine him into something greater than he was, but that was my own fault. I hadn't managed my expectations and momentarily lost sight of why I was online dating to begin with. Even though there were no hard feelings from the date, Granny is an avid cheerleader on my team and felt the urge to pep me up.

"Kid, you are beautiful, you are intelligent, you deserve to be with someone fantastic—"

"Granny!" I cut her off. "I'm totally cool. It wasn't horrible, it just wasn't mind-blowing."

"You deserve mind-blowing. Oy, don't we all," she commiserated. "Listen, all I have to say to you is you go girl, you go!"

With my ego nicely massaged, I changed gears to get the scoop on her phone chat. "So tell me! When are you meeting him?"

"Who-oo-oo-oo? The stu-ut-ut-ter-er?" she asked with a repetitive staccato for each syllable.

I didn't get it. She laughed like a schoolyard bully. "This guy could barely get through a sentence! He has a stutter like you wouldn't believe."

"Granny," I scolded, "he was probably just nervous. It was his first time talking to you, and you're very intimidating."

"Me? No way," she joked. I've known my ball-busting granny for more than twenty-four years. It is a miracle that I haven't developed a stutter.

"It's apparent why he's hiding behind a computer," she huffed.

"Granny!"

"Listen, I was very polite. He called when I was in the car driving by the Gardens Mall, we talked for a little bit, then the old fart got worried that I wasn't capable of driving and talking on my phone at the same time. Who the hell does he think I am?"

I know exactly who he thinks she is, and he's right. Granny loves having her cell phone attached to her ear as she cruises through South Florida. Driving with her is a terrifying experience where you cling to the handlebar and cringe as she honks at other drivers, lowering her window to trash-talk if they pull a move she doesn't find kosher.

The lady cuts people off, zips through red lights, and takes pleasure in yelling creative profanities out her window. One time I was driving with her when a man pulled in front of us. Granny followed on his tail for three lights until she finally caught up to him, then signaled him to roll down the window. "What are you, sick?" she asked. He shook his head, confused by the old woman leaning halfway out of her car.

"Well, you gotta be sick to pull a move like that." The light turned green and she floored it, speeding away.

"Mmmhmm"—I avoided the subject—"and then what?" I asked.

"Then he said he'd call me next week."

"Well, stutter aside, did he seem nice? Will you go get a drink with him?" I asked.

"A drink? I'm gonna need two drinks, *at least*, if I'm going to go out with him, but sure. Why not? Maybe a drink will loosen him up. You know, I *am* open to new things."

So she said . . . Granny almost had me fooled into believing she was being rational about going out with a potential suitor. She was as cool as a cucumber, until the day of the date. I received two phone calls and four frantic voice mails all before noon. The little prima donna tried to pull every excuse in the book to weasel her way out of the date.

First it was work stuff: "I have an early morning tomorrow. I need today to prepare." Then it was the restaurant he chose: "The service is slow; all those teenyboppers in fluorescent T-shirts just sit in the back and pick their noses." When those excuses didn't work, she kicked it up a notch and moved on to inflicting/making up injuries: "I smashed my foot into my bedroom door, I'm gushing blood between my toes. I should go to the emergency room. This is a gash, kid. I need stitches!" I didn't have to be there to know that the worst thing that could have happened was she stubbed a toe.

Her devious behavior reminded me of the desperate excuses I would fabricate to stay home from school on the day of a big test that I wasn't prepared for. I listened to her whine for a bit, as she did for me, then told her to suck it up and pick out an outfit.

She called back. "You won't believe this." I already didn't. "I opened the kitchen cabinet and smashed my nose. Blood. Everywhere. More stitches. I'm going to have a black eye, I know it!"

I wished I could have been there to calm her down or at least watch the Marx Brothers–esque physical comedy that was supposedly occurring in her apartment. I suggested that she was being dramatic, which only set her off further. "I need a pep talk! I need support! I don't need any of your snarky judgments," she hollered.

She was right. As a granddaughter and wingman I needed to calm her down then pep her up. After the uncomfortable nerves of my first date, I had every reason to be sympathetic to Granny. Although she'd never admit it, that little lady needed me more than I needed her. I had to remind her why we were doing this. Her evening could totally blow and it still would be a success because it would be an experience that took her out of her comfort zone and brought her one step away from Ira. I reminded her of all the qualities she liked on his profile: he had a great job; he was a family man; he was well read and had traveled the world. He also had a boat. Who doesn't love a boat ride?

The tension in her voice began to soften. "All right, I'm thinking I'm gonna go casual chic, you know some cute flat sandals, a pair of capris, and a little top I got from Banana Republic two years ago for fifty percent off." Nothing calms her nerves like a good deal.

I oohed and aahed in support, then suggested we choose a mantra for her to chant for confidence. "How about 'I'm gonna marry him, I'm gonna marry him'?" she suggested, then burst into a fit of nervous laughter.

I wasn't going to rain on her wedding, but it's smarter to

stick with a more realistic motto. "How about 'The best thing that happens is you fall in love, the worst thing that happens is we laugh about it after'?"

She thought for a second; I could feel her coming around. "Yeah, yeah, love or laughs, it's all good stuff." She repeated it a few times, gaining more confidence with each go. "All right, kid, you did good."

After clearly defining our intentions and managing expectations, I felt good about sending Granny out on her first date. She chose to break her seal on the scene with Tim, a cheeky man who told her, "I'm happy to take your virginity—in online dating."

Tim was a smooth operator. The nerves he felt on their phone chat must have been calmed because in person his stutter was gone and his ego was back in full force. When she pecked him on the cheek in greeting, he said, "That kiss is gonna have to get a little more serious, sweetheart." Then he asked how she would like it if her hair were blowing around in a convertible.

"Why, am I buying a convertible?" she asked.

"No, but I have a red Jaguar that you'll be riding in." Tim was laying down some heavy game. Bow-chicka-wow-wow.

I called to get the scoop two hours after her date began. Based on her earlier freak out, I imagined she would suck down a quick glass of wine then make some wild excuse to bail. To my surprise, when she answered the phone she politely told me she'd have to call back. Her tone of voice was so sweet and foreign I thought there was a chance some other granny had stolen her phone.

Her date lasted *four* hours! I know my granny. If she doesn't want to be in a situation she'll find her way out of it. Although he sounded smart and interesting, Granny is a tough judge. She picked him apart from his ruddy fingernails to his slight case of tremors. I suspected her criticisms were born out of a defensive place of managing future expectations and protecting herself by finding his faults before he found hers. Although she did plenty of post-date kvetching, I had a hunch she secretly enjoyed herself.

Tim was very confident but perhaps too confident. In her recap she complained incessantly about his self-indulgent manner of talking about himself. She said, "He never shuts up, he talked the entire time. I wanted to say, 'Have a glass of water, my God.'" Granny has a freakishly similar habit.

Even though Tim put down some solid moves, Granny wasn't going to be wooed so easily. When I asked why she was so hesitant to commit or simply let herself go, she said, "I had one man in my life where I ate when he was hungry, slept when he was tired, and went where he wanted to go." It was going to take some work getting my fiercely independent granny adjusted to the idea of a companion.

# Settling for Life

**W**HEN GRANNY GOT HITCHED the year was 1954. Just trying to imagine what it was like to be a woman in that era is frustrating. "At seventeen, eighteen, nineteen, you were serious about your dating situation," she told me. "Same as now when you're going out at twenty-eight, twenty-nine, thirty." If the same rules applied to my generation and I had married any of the losers I dated in my late teens (like my high school boyfriend, Brian, the college drop-out who played in a band and lived in his parents' pool house with aspirations to make it big as a reality TV star), I suspect I would have turned out to be a resentful mom and wife with a subscription to Ashley Madison and an addiction to QVC and cupcakes.

The simplest way for me to wrap my head around Granny's marital situation was to compare her to Betty Draper in *Mad Men*. They were both adulterous housewives who were bored out of their minds. They married because it was the easiest option. "Five weeks, Kayli. We were dating for five weeks before we got married," she said. Her husband provided a beautiful home in a nice neighborhood and all the other props that created the facade of happiness. She went from being a young girl to a mother and wife all before entering her twenties. Cooking, cleaning, entertaining, child rearing . . . it was all fine and good, but she wanted more out of life.

I never gave marriage much consideration until I arrived, utterly single, at the stage in my midtwenties where at least one person a week was showing up in my Facebook news feed as "engaged."

A month into my OkCupid journey, one of my closest gal pals, Caitlin, invited me to her bridal shower. I had a minimeltdown. I wasn't ready for marriage yet. What the hell was everyone doing? Weren't we too young? What's next? Mortgages? Children? Spider veins? No sir.

Charlie and I had talked about marriage a lot. I guess I had blindly assumed that we'd eventually take the plunge, but when it came time to talk logistics, I couldn't wrap my head around it. The party sounded nice. I imagined it would be at his family's farm or on top of a castle we visited in Spain. There'd be a mariachi band and red velvet cupcakes. I would obviously have two dresses, a classy lace number for the ceremony and a saucy cream mini for the party. I could only grasp the wedding in my head, a picturesque event that would take place in the far-off future. Everything that came after throwing the bouquet was off my radar.

Granny's holy matrimony began when she and Mark tied the knot in downtown New York at one of the many Jewish catering places that used to dominate the area. "My father-in-law invited everyone he met on the subway that morning," she said. I could hear the long-standing regret in her voice. "I had bought a white lace dress that came tight at the waist that I was planning on wearing in the Catskills to a dance at Grossinger's Hotel with my girlfriends in June. I never made it to the dance." Six weeks later she was pregnant with my mom and there was no turning back.

Two years into their marriage, her husband came home from a business trip and she could tell something was off. He wouldn't make eye contact. He cowered at her touch. "I have to tell you something," Mark confessed. "There were girls at the retreat."

"So?" she asked naively.

"They were brought in to *entertain*," he admitted shamefully. His guilty conscience got the better of him. He cheated but chose to come clean. Unlike many men of his era (to be fair, probably all eras) who felt no conscience about adulterous behavior, he loved her too much to live in guilt.

I was shocked when she told me about his confession. I imagined it would have been beyond crushing as a young wife to learn of your husband's infidelities. "Eh," she huffed, "to be honest, I didn't care. It made me realize that although I may have *loved* him I was not *in love* with him. If I was I would have been jealous as hell, but I wasn't." I saw her point. If the thought of her man with another woman didn't make her blood boil, there had to be something major missing in their relationship.

That incident served as a wake-up call. Just because her husband wasn't the love of her life didn't mean she wasn't going to have one. A year later she met Ira and started up her own affair — one that she did *not* confess to her husband. Although her twenty-two-year-long marriage was full of lies, discontentment, and failed expectations, she was too afraid to give it up. It was a cowardly move, but she felt that she was better off with him than without him. It wasn't like today where a woman has endless options. She was financially dependent on her husband and there was no feasible way out.

This was the environment that my mom, an only child, was raised in. In response, as a wife herself, she made it a point to always have the means to support her independence. My parents got divorced when I was six. My mom wasn't going to stick around in a loveless marriage like she watched her mother do. She left my father and went on to essentially raise my sisters and me on her own.

I remember my mom telling me the story of her wedding day when I was a kid. I didn't hear about dancing and cake, I heard about her hyperventilating in the bathroom before she walked down the aisle, knowing she was making the wrong decision.

I grew up adjusted to the idea that marriage doesn't always last forever. I've been suspicious of the institution for as long as I can recall.

"You only get married for the first time once" was the title of a Facebook album posted for Caitlin's bridal shower. The gal who put it together had an especially twisted sense of humor. Albeit dark, she managed to sum up the pessimistic feelings of the event in one snappy caption.

You only get married for the second time once too. My mother's take two with marriage took place on the back of a donkey in Cancun.

It was the year before my Bat Mitzvah (as if I didn't have big enough things to stress about—my dress, torah portion, and party theme). I was thirteen and at summer camp when I received a postcard—a photo of my mom and her then boyfriend on the back of an ass, both smiling at the camera and holding up their fingers to show off their shiny new bands.

The back of the picture read "Just Married!" Way to trauma-tize a kid, Mom.

Luckily for all of us, by the time they came back to the States their tequila hangover and marriage had both dissolved. If I had a therapist I feel like she might point to this event as the moment when I realized how fleeting marriage could be.

When it came to Caitlin getting married, I was ecstatic for her and thrilled to be a part of the celebration. She is per-fect, her man is terrific, I hope they live happily ever after, yadda yadda yadda. The foreboding Facebook album slogan was something I took more personally for my life and future partner(s). The bridal "party" was filled with talk of discon-tentment and sexless relationships. There were whispers of in-fidelity, boredom, and uncertainty. My grandmother's marital problems were not issues from yesteryear; they very much car-ried over to modern-day relationships.

It was shocking to hear some of the beautiful young women reveal that they weren't getting laid by their spouses— *not* because they didn't want it but because their men didn't want to give it. (The Facebook album creator, a recent divor-cée, revealed that her one-year marriage fell apart when she began bullying her husband by flicking his flaccid penis and pretending it was a microphone. She'd tap it and say, "Is this thing on?")

When it was time to open presents the guests all oohed and aahed at the kitchen tools that were masquerading as gifts. Someone even gave Caitlin a spatula with her future last name etched into the wooden handle.

"If it doesn't work out," one of the pessimistic gals whis-pered in my ear, "there's enough room for her to engrave 'For-mer' before his last name." Big shocker, I was the only one who bought sex toys. I assumed that a cheeky necklace that doubled as a vibrator would be a hit, but the crowd all went nuts for the garlic cutter instead.

The word "settle" was thrown around quite a bit. That word makes my throat close up and my hands get clammy. Deep down I am terrified of dying alone in a bed surrounded by cats and dolls (I don't own either but who knows how weird I'll get with age). Settling is something I refuse to do. One of the girls declared that Mr. Right doesn't exist; she insisted that we should be looking to acquire a harem of men, each with a quality we value: Mr. Fix-It, Mr. Romantic, Mr. Funny, Mr. Kinky, Mr. Chef, Mr. Rich, and Mr. Tattoos. It's impossible, she argued, to find one man with all these qualities, or at least none of these gals or myself had found him yet.

Granny is always trying to hustle babies out of me, but a ring on my finger was far from anything I had ever heard her promote. I called her after Caitlin's bridal shower and asked her stance on marriage. The phone went silent, then after gathering her thoughts she said, "I need great-grandkids, I know that. You gotta give them to me before I die. Marriage, eh, that's a gray area."

"I don't think it's for me," I declared. Those girls had really freaked me out. I was scared of being locked into an unhappy relationship that would only get more complicated over time with the added mess of babies, bills, and history. How would I ever find someone who I could love and would love me back for a *lifetime*? When the institution of marriage was first created our life expectancy was roughly thirty-two; now we're expected to live happily ever after with *one* person until we're in our *nineties*?

"Life changes people," she told me. "Do you think there's

one couple that got married and forty years later—four decades!—they're still the same to each other and they still have the same feelings? It might still be love but it will be different. Other things are more important than in the beginning. If you expect it to be the same you're fooling yourself," she warned.

I grunted. I was trying to swallow a big pill.

"Listen, you know the Brad Pitt and Angela Whatchamacallit? They have a kennel full of kids but no vows exchanged. Now their children want them to seal the deal. I don't think it matters what order you do it in, but I think eventually you have to take the plunge. You meet a guy that you're suited with, you understand each other, you love each other, you want the same things, you certainly must have sexual chemistry—you just do it. No promises that it'll last forever, but what the hell lasts forever anyway?"

It was refreshing to hear Granny, a lady who never had luck in her own marriage, stand behind the institution. "My advice," she said. "Be sure, be sure, be sure, be sure, because with all that assuredness you still can't be sure, but if you look for pitfalls and don't ignore them, you have a better chance."

I admit that the idea of Mr. Right is naively optimistic. Deep down I know the soul mate scenario is a fairy tale, but that doesn't mean I'd ever quit holding out hope. Truth is, there *have* been and *will* be many men who are right for me at different times in my life. Charlie was right for me when I met him, but people change. Like she said, nothing is permanent.

I was ready to meet my harem: Mr. Adventure, Mr. Artist, what the hell, maybe even Mr. S&M. The more men I met, the more I would be able to define what it was I wanted in a partner, which would only help in making me more *sure* when my *next* Mr. Right decided to come along.

# Fantastic vs. Farty

**P**ART OF THE NATURE of posting a sexy shot for your profile pic while living in a highly populated city is receiving at least a dozen messages a day to weed through. Most of the emails in my inbox lacked any creativity, suggesting we meet for "a drink" or alerting me to what a "babe" I am. Tell me something I don't know.

Post–bridal shower, I wanted to go out with someone more my speed. When I got a message from Christophe, a self-proclaimed movie buff, I was intrigued. He invited me to see *Drive,* the new Ryan Gosling movie. I was impressed that he got straight to the point and suggested something that, although not wildly imaginative, I actually wanted to do.

Rather than meeting up at the theater and going straight in, we decided to grab some coffee at the crowded Think Coffee café near Union Square to get acquainted before the film. I spotted Christophe anxiously pacing in front of the glass doors. I recognized him from his pictures and gave a polite wave as I approached. He nodded at me and shook my hand like a busy CEO as we walked in. I ordered a latte. Christophe declined a beverage, shaking his hands in the air when he told me he was already "wired." He wasn't lying. In thirty minutes Christophe rattled off his entire life history of growing up in France and attending private boarding schools; about his sister and her three children, his fear of bicycles, a solo trip to Latvia, and quitting it all to pursue filmmaking in New York. *Whoosh.*

He had just completed a film summer intensive at NYU, the same program I had my degree from. That was something I was attracted to from his profile. I wanted to be around a creative individual who had the potential to inspire me to get back into my moviemaking passion.

As we strolled to the theater I asked about his work, influences, and plans—he was crazy excited to share every detail of his life and opinions with me. At first hearing Christophe talk about film was refreshing; he got so fired up and animated on the subject he was literally stumbling on words, trying to get them out of his mouth. He was clearly a nerd, but a passionate nerd, which *can* be endearing.

We settled into the theater as the lights came down and the trailers started rolling. He nudged me at the first one. "I love this director, great work," he said loud enough for the people in front of us to turn and look. "He's my favorite," he exclaimed at the next trailer. When the film began I shifted toward the elderly stranger on my left, trying to pretend I was with him so the bitchy teenage girls in front of us would stop turning around to gawk at me.

"Ooh, great lighting!" he practically shouted. The guy next to Christophe scowled in his direction. He didn't notice; he was too busy foaming at the mouth from excitement. "Amazing score, I love this soundtrack," "Great effects, that blood looks real. What do you think they used?" "What else is she in?" "Nice editing, are you familiar with this editor?" By that point I was basically crawling into the guy next to me's lap. It was like sitting in a film class except we weren't in school and he wasn't teaching me anything. After the credits rolled I politely thanked him for the movie and went on my way. I liked the film a lot; he liked it more.

I vented to Granny about Christophe, but she didn't seem to hear anything about his annoying film-school commentary or his keyed up personality. After I had a good rant she said, "Let me get this straight: he went to boarding school, a prestigious university, he's been all over the world, he's close with his family, worked in finance *internationally*, and now has the means to fool around with a camera? He's clearly intelligent and very wealthy. He sounds fantastic, but okay, fantastic isn't what you're after? That's fine, you're twenty-four, you're probably not ready for fantastic."

That sounded like a dare to me. *Fantastic? I'm ready for fantastic. Show me fantastic,* I thought. To me, Christophe wasn't fantastic. Just because you share common interests with someone doesn't make you a match. If I stuck with him for his appearance on paper, I would be settling and risking the possibility of ending up at my own bridal shower getting giddy over a spatula. I *refused* to settle.

I put the same pressure on Granny. "You wouldn't know what fantastic was if it hit you in the face," I bullied.

"I've had fantastic. Men at this age are farty, not fantastic," she huffed. I still had a long way to go in squashing her cynical side. She certainly wasn't gallivanting around with any fresh studs.

I began to pry. "What's going on with Mike?"

Granny let out an exasperated moan. Mike was a silver fox who sent a message the previous week: "You have very cute grandkids." Naturally I liked him.

Mike had an MBA from Yale, lived in Palm Beach (originally from the Northeast), was an avid eater, passionate traveler, and highly capable of composing a lively profile. Granny was into it. We agonized for twenty minutes over what to write in her reply. Should she be coy and make him wait a few days? Should she be witty or provocative? Should she compliment his grandkids even though they didn't look as cute as hers?

We kept it short, sweet, and sassy, just like Granny. Two days went by and no word from Mike. Trying to avoid any hurt feelings, in typical Granny fashion, she was prepared to write him off. "Probably fell off his wheelchair and died," she concluded.

I explained that it was a modern world, and given that he provided his number and *encouraged* her to call, there was no shame in giving him a ring. After plenty of pouting she sucked it up and took the plunge. They played a quick game of phone tag before she finally got him on the line. "He sounded withdrawn and uncomfortable, as if somebody else, possibly a persistent grandchild, was encouraging him to be online dating," she told me. He alluded to there being a recent change in his life. "I think his wife just died and somebody else wrote his profile and messages," she said. "I really feel it, I feel it in my gut and I'm a bit of a witch." (Whenever Granny wants to drive home a point she brings up her supposed sorceress psychic ability.)

"It's not all fun and games, kid. Old people carry a lot of baggage and reservations that make this whole process quite difficult. Let's face it, they get their juices running on the computer because they can't do it in real life."

She was receiving several messages from random men in faraway states like Washington and North Dakota; clearly they weren't looking for a viable relationship with a senior in South Florida. I felt for Granny. I knew she wasn't looking for a soul mate, but I also knew that with the added past and angst that people of her generation carry, it was going to be a struggle for her to find a kindred spirit to crack her shell.

As a younger gal looking in, it seems many older folks assume they've already experienced the most thrilling parts of their lives and had their most valuable relationships. They're not worried about meeting the loves of their lives; they're looking for some entertainment or watered-down version of company. Although that sounds grim, I think it should be taken as an exciting opportunity. The pressure is off to find Mr. Right, develop a family, or share a mortgage with someone. Yes, there is history, but now that all the heavy stuff has passed, why not just concentrate on having good times?

When I asked Granny if she was going to give up, she said, "What, are you calling me a loser? Give me a break. No way. For every fifty guys you get I'll get one. I'll go with the flow, weed out the strange ones, and see where this all goes." Thata girl, Granny. To add more fish to Granny's senior pool, I built an additional profile for her on Match.com.

I had to admire her positive attitude. It was contagious. If she could have the chutzpah so could I.

# Liar, Liar, Pants on Fire!

I WAS BROWSING THE HUNKS of OkCupid one pro-crastination-filled afternoon when an instant message popped up from Globetrot66: "Hey, what's your story?" "Where do you want me to start?" I replied.

"What do you do?"

It felt like an odd question to start a conversation with. I understand that what someone does is a big part of who they are, but I don't think it should define them. I danced around the question because my answer felt too long and drawn out for an introductory IM chat.

"A lot of things, what about you?" I guardedly replied.

"Corporate law, where you from?"

We bantered back and forth until Globetrot66, AKA Paul, was thoroughly charmed by my ambiguous banter. He suggested we get a drink, an invitation to get to know each other off the web. Paul's profile had attracted me because: a) it stated that he was six feet three inches, and b) it included an in-depth declaration about his love and frequency of travel. He even went so far as to specify his passport as the number one thing he could not live without.

I'm a lady who loves adventure. Charlie and I traveled to

nine countries together in four years—camping, climbing, kayaking, biking, straight-up living. I needed to find a partner who could hang with me like that. I indulged myself, imagining Paul and me trekking through Patagonia, cheering each other along as I stared up into his adoring eyes (a good eight inches above my own). Oh, the escapades ahead of us . . .

Unfortunately, it turned out he was not a traveler, not even a vacationer; it would have been a stretch to call him a weekender. He was a corporate lawyer with a flesh-toned beard (it was too pale to spot in his picture) who clocked in at around five-ten. It is rude and close-minded to judge someone based on his or her job, but Paul felt no qualms about stereotyping me so I paid him the same respect.

As soon as I sat down at the stuffy Midtown bar that Paul chose, he wanted to talk work. The place was filled with young professionals having after-work cocktails. All the men looked like carbon copies of Paul. With his BlackBerry (in my opinion, the number one thing he could not live without) clutched in his hand, he told me all about his hectic day in the office while frequently taking breaks to scroll through emails and shake his head at the beloved phone.

Once we exhausted all the thrills of mergers and acquisitions, the spotlight was on me. I went into my film school background and the nonprofit I founded. Then I dropped the bomb: "I also work in a nightclub."

Paul shifted in his seat; behind his translucent whiskers I saw his mouth smirk with a sense of superiority. "What, are you a dancer?" he asked with a smug tone. I've seen this reaction from men before, and I knew what was coming next.

Of course a rigid corporate lawyer like Paul would jump to that assumption. Although I occasionally attempted an awkward bop to the beat, I don't think anyone would call my off-rhythm movements dancing. I just served drinks. "Well, you must get into some seriously shady situations. Do you drink every night? I bet you do a lot of drugs, huh? What do they make you wear? Have you ever gotten laid at work? Has anyone ever made you an offer you couldn't refuse?"

"Paul," I said, trying my hardest not to snap, "I sell alcohol not sex."

I took a deep breath, then tried to answer each question eloquently and articulately to assure him that I wasn't the working gal he had in mind. I explained that I didn't work in nightlife for my health or to dance on tables shaking sparklers like a proud patriot. The nightclub is a means to an end and sustains all the much more interesting aspects of my life. I tried to bring the conversation back to my other pursuits.

Paul didn't give a damn. He wanted to hear something much more salacious than I had to offer. He was being just as disrespectful as the douche-bag patrons I loathe in the club. I felt like I was on trial defending myself. If Paul were my boyfriend I might have allowed some of his prying questions, but he was a stranger and I was getting ready to pull out his beige face hair.

I very obviously tried to change the subject. "*So*, tell me about where you've been traveling recently."

He scratched his head. "Me and some buddies went to Boston in May," the self-dubbed Globetrot66 began. I nodded encouragingly. "Yeah, we went to some soccer game. It was pretty lame."

"Anywhere else?"

"I flew to London for work about two years ago. It was pretty cool. Haven't really done much traveling since college though, been busy with work, stuck behind the desk, you know?" he said. I sensed some sarcasm in his tone.

He was letting me down left and right. London? Two years ago? For work? I wanted stories about monks in Asia and shark diving in South Africa. He was not a "Globetrot66." To be fair, to Paul I was not a philanthropist or filmmaker, I was just a cocktail waitress.

Before I could end the date, Paul took the honor. Less than forty-five minutes after we sat down, he scooted out his chair, did a dramatic time check on his beloved BlackBerry, and suggested that it was getting late. It wasn't even 8 p.m.

At first I was in shock, my ego almost bruised that this guy didn't want to spend more time with me. I *obviously* wasn't into him—but still! The nerve of this corporate lawyer! Then he said, "So maybe I'll text you sometime if I want to get into that club you work at."

I laughed in his face. "That is an offer I'm definitely going to have to refuse." The idea of seeing Paul for another five minutes at that bar, let alone the bar I work at, was something I absolutely did not want. When online dating, you need to check your ego at the door; some people will not like you and you won't like some people, that's just the way things work on- and offline. I kissed Paul good-bye on the cheek, then immediately regretted it once I felt his shiny whiskers against my lips.

I needed Granny. "An asshole and on top of it a bore? I can't believe you didn't sock him in the face. Forget him," she instructed.

I would have loved to forget him, but annoyingly Paul wouldn't let me. I thought we clearly ended things but the punk had the nerve to text me at 1 a.m. the following two nights after our date: "What r u doin?"

First off, if you're too lazy to type full three-letter words, I already think you're an idiot, but more important, his timing and choice to message me after how we ended things was beyond repulsive.

"The man has no tact," Granny said. "Next! You need someone more artsy craftsy, you know? Someone who can relate to you and your lifestyle. Maybe someone who works with their hands. But no starving artists—at the very least a middle-of-the-road artist."

I agreed. I didn't want someone who had to stretch the truth on his profile about the type of guy he'd *like* to be. I needed to find a man who understood my lifestyle, accepted me for who I was, and was comfortable enough in his own skin that he wouldn't need to put me down to feel better about himself.

Next up was John, a quirky-looking guy with gorgeous baby blues. His profile seemed to fit Granny's description. He was an art director and played in a band—isn't that exactly what she meant by a middle-of-the-road artist?

Prior to meeting, John and I exchanged some messages that at the time seemed funny but looking back were just weird. Example:

> **Him:** Hey there, you have a lovely smile and pretty
>     coordinated red motif in your photo. How's your
>     weekend going?
> **Me:** Thanks for noticing the red, it really means a
>     lot. Sorry I've been away for a few weeks, but this
>     weekend happens to be going well! How is yours?
> **Him:** Weekend went swimmingly . . . pun intended.
>     The ocean can be a wonderful place when it's not the
>     middle of October in 1991.

**Me:** October '91 . . . I'm guessing some shit went down? Wanna talk about it?

He was clearly an oddball, but he was also an artist and artists tend to be eccentric. I could be open to eccentricities . . . He suggested Turks and Frogs, a cozy wine bar in the West Village, to get an after-work drink.

Meeting new people or entering foreign situations typically doesn't arouse feelings of anxiety in me. I tend to do well in social affairs. Granny says it's because I'm gregarious and my confidence is on the border of arrogance. This all might be true. However, in the first moments of an OkCupid date, the ragingly proud guido fist pumping in my heart bowed down and a nervous nutcase came out. It felt like walking into an interview, and all the same panicked thoughts went through my head: *Will he like me? Am I dressed appropriately? What is he going to ask? Do I shake hands or kiss on cheek? Do I have sweat stains? Why am I talking in a voice that's at least two pitches above my regular tone?*

Because I experienced the initial predate jitters, I tried to be empathetic to my online suitors.

When I arrived at the bar I did a scan over the meager crowd to see if he was there. No such luck. I took a seat on a stool and ordered a beer like a pro. As I was paying I looked out the window and saw a very nervous man talking to himself as he paced back and forth three times before opening the door and walking in. At first I thought he might be a schizophrenic lunatic, but it turned out it was John, my date.

He must have seen me when he walked in since there were only about six other people at the bar including the bartender and a busboy. My nerves manifested into a stiff, teethy grin. I waved at him but he didn't approach me. Instead he stood on

the opposite side of the room, ordered a ginger ale, then focused his eyes firmly on the floor. I would have doubted that
it was in fact John, but he was wearing the same bright-check-
ered shirt as his profile picture, so I felt pretty certain.

I took a deep breath, swallowed my inhibitions, hopped
off my stool, and approached him. "Hey, John?" I tapped him
on the shoulder. He looked up at me like I was an old work
colleague who he wanted to avoid. I went in for my signature
double-cheek kiss/hug/handshake; I still hadn't mastered the
appropriate greeting.

I suggested we move to a table and take a seat. John quietly
sipped his ginger ale like a seven-year-old boy, staring at the
straw intently. I half expected him to blow bubbles. "So you
work over here? You like music? You play in a band? Where'd
you go to school? What happened in October of 1991?" I went
through a series of get-to-know-you questions. He murmured
three word answers back. The tables were turned, except I
didn't feel like an interviewer because then I would be talking to an adult; I felt more like a guidance counselor trying to
gently coax answers out of a painfully shy child.

John was surprisingly attractive, and being that he was
thirty-three, I couldn't figure out how he could possibly be
so socially inept. I briefly considered how important conversation would be in my future relationship. Maybe John was
just a quiet thinker, an artist full of eccentricities. Maybe we
would just sit silently and create things together. He was a
musician too; maybe he'd use music to express his feelings.

I tried to make eye contact, but every time his baby
blues met mine he shifted uncomfortably and turned away.
It seemed odd to me that he could have the confidence to
be in a band and get onstage in front of an audience, but he
couldn't let his eyes meet mine, and for some reason he was

repeatedly referring to me as "dude" and/or "man," which I assume meant either he was super nervous by my stunning presence or he thought I resembled someone from the male species and it made him uncomfortable.

"So tell me about your band," I pushed on.

"U-uh," he stuttered, "it's not really a band. I just play the guitar, but it's—it's not to get girls . . . it's . . . uh . . . dude . . . it's more just for me."

To bust his balls I brought up the fact that his profile picture is of him holding his guitar. He didn't appreciate this reminder. "I'm on the—the YouTube," he told me, "but I don't have too many hits. I'm mainly trying to keep my stuff on the DL for now, man."

I nodded solemnly. "Do you live near here?" He shifted, then stiffly nodded. "Where?" I asked.

"Just across the river." His profile listed him as a New Yorker. Across the river is New Jersey, not New York, and certainly not the West Village. "Dude, I like it out there because I have a lot of space, a whole floor actually."

Okay, that sounded kind of cool. I started picturing a high-rise with Manhattan views, modern architecture, and slick marble countertops. "Any roommates?" I asked.

"Just my mom," he said. "She lives downstairs. It's her house. But I have the whole upstairs." If I were in high school this would have sounded like a pretty sweet setup, but as a self-sufficient modern lady, this wasn't the most appealing of living scenarios for a potential beau.

John was wearing me down. "Have you gotten out of the city at all this summer?" I asked.

"Yeah, dude. I went to Maine with my buddy. It was like *Brokeback Mountain*," he said.

"Things got a little gay?" I joked.

His cheeks brightened as he shifted a few more times. He looked beyond offended by my comment. "No, it was just very outdoorsy," he said.

Both of our glasses were empty. I made the executive decision to save the calorie count by wrapping up and heading out. Just like in an interview, I thanked John for coming to meet me and said I'd be in touch. We went in for our final cheek kiss/hug/handshake maneuver and walked our separate ways.

My conclusion for the date was either: a) he didn't like me, or b) he liked me so much it made him nervous. I decided to go with b because it fit my ego better.

I'm all about spontaneity, but one of the advantages of online dating versus real-world meeting is the ability to interact and do more research before committing to a date. It was becoming clear that I needed to do my homework; I wanted to be more discerning before taking the dive to meet an online suitor in the flesh.

When I whined to Granny about John and his jittery and peculiar behavior topped off with his list of lies, she switched into Jewish grandmother mode—a setting she can't fight. Don't they all want us to marry doctors and lawyers? After some reflection she came at me with second thoughts on Paul the corporate lawyer. A lawyer has a handsome income and Granny has a touch of an old-fashioned gal in her. Although I know she wants me to make my own money, she loves the idea of someone setting me up in a big ole house and showering me in rubies.

"Maybe you should give him a second chance?" she coyly suggested.

I reminded her of how rude he was to me and that he

looked like Spencer Pratt. I was onto her. "You want me to go out with him again just because he's a lawyer."

She feigned shock and immediately jumped to the defense. "No, that's not it. You're not a lawyer kind of date person," she insisted, practicing some of her legendary reverse psychology on me. "I'm just saying, you could develop a *special* relationship. I don't want you to marry a lawyer, you'd end up divorcing a lawyer."

"He called me at one a.m.!"

"Maybe he's a night owl. Maybe he was working late and wanted to grab a late-night snack," she hypothesized.

"I know what he wanted to snack on . . ."

No grandmother wants her granddaughter getting shady calls from shady men past midnight. "Eh, fine. Screw him — not literally," she said.

"Thank you."

In a last-ditch effort she quietly suggested, "I just think he might have made those calls because he liked you too much. Some men don't know how to deal with those feelings."

"Granny, whose team are you on?"

"Oy, okay, okay, cool it."

# This Ain't Her First Rodeo

GRANNY HAS WHAT IT TAKES to be a cougar. She has style, sass, and a slight aversion to older gentlemen that could easily work its way into a healthy appetite for a youthful boy toy.

When Jake, *another* self-proclaimed lover of travel, asked Granny out for a drink, I told her I wouldn't entertain any kvetching. "I don't want to hear anything from you until you meet him face-to-face," I instructed.

"He hasn't even asked for a phone call yet. I should just meet a man without talking to him first?" she asked.

"No one talks on the phone anymore," I naively told her, lapsing on my new emphasis on predate research. "You're going out with him."

Moments after her date wrapped she called me and proposed the question: "What's wrong with this picture?" She was about to let me have it. "When I have to say to the gentleman who took me out, 'Please call me when you get home so I know you got there safely.' What would you say the problem is?"

I considered, concluding she was referring to his age. "He's an older man, you're an older woman. This I know. Give me some real juice," I said.

"Listen, all I'm saying is, I don't like going out with a man that I gotta worry if he's dead or alive," she said defensively. "But okay, so I get there and he's not five-six; he lied, he's probably five-two, but he was wearing cowboy boots that propped him up an extra inch or two. He dressed well for an older gentleman, some nice trousers, with a crease. I love a crease—"

I was stuck on the cowboy boots. September in Florida is way too hot for that much foot/ankle coverage. "Oh yeah," she grunted. "He sure loves them boots. He spent a good hour enlightening me on his boot maintenance. He's got six pairs. Once a month he lines them all up and spit polishes them—whatever the hell that means. He leaves the black for last because they take the most work. Jesus."

After drinks they continued on to another restaurant for dinner. Like I experienced with Robert, she didn't know how to end the date. Their outing clocked in at over four hours. She said he was a very nice man, attentive, gentlemanly, and kind, but he didn't have a sense of humor to keep her captivated. "I wanna laugh; if I can't laugh it's not worth it." I couldn't argue with that. I'd rather date a funny guy than a stud any day.

Jake did share Granny's passion for travel, just not the same method of transport or level of comfort. "He loves RVing, especially at Yellowstone Park. He was really doing a hard sell to get me on board. I said, 'Whaddaya crazy? You drive there. Fly me out, I'll stop in to say hello. Or let's take your RV to Paris and park it in front a nice hotel in the Champs-Élysées.'"

"You princess."

"Kid, can you imagine eating breakfast, lunch, and dinner in an RV? No way. The best part of traveling is enjoying the local flavors and cuisines." I pictured my stuck-up Granny making it twenty miles or so, then asking to be dropped off at the nearest outlet mall.

The lady has ridiculously high standards. Ira spoiled her rotten when it came to travel. The deceiving duo hit almost every continent, big city, and exotic beach on the globe. After each trip, before returning to New York, they'd spend a night at a hotel across from Notre Dame in Paris. "It was our spot, our routine," she told me. My envy was obviously off the charts. I wouldn't mind having that sort of routine in my life.

Even though Granny wasn't wildly impressed with Jake or his RV, it didn't slow him down. He called the next day to invite her out for a rib dinner at some veterans' club that he's a member of. "You should go!" I encouraged.

"Ribs? At a veterans' club? Please, there is a time and a place for ribs. This is not it. Besides I'm sure there's going to be square dancing—it's all the rage for the old people down here to square dance. No ribs and no square dancing for me," she said. It's frustrating but also comforting that Granny is so adamant in what she likes and what she doesn't.

It seemed as though our efforts to maintain mystery in our profiles were only hindering our success on the sites. Besides withholding details online, I was hesitant to share my new hobby with friends. I don't care what the magazines say; there is still a touch of stigma to online dating for the "uninitiated," even if it is self-inflicted. Over lunch with some girlfriends in Fort Greene, I cautiously revealed my dirty little dating secret.

I paused, expecting to hear gasps, giggles, and teasing, but I didn't get any of that. In fact, their reactions were almost annoyingly underwhelming and accepting.

One friend, a gorgeous Swedish dancer, revealed that she was dating someone she met on Match.com and had several successful dates on the site before settling on her current beau. Another reminded me that our friend Sarah, a blond British babe, was still dating the guy she met on OkCupid in the fall. "Hate to break it to you, but online dating isn't as taboo as you think."

Okay, so I was being a wimp. Granny and I were not pioneers of Internet love. I reluctantly showed my dancer friend my profile and only then did the mocking begin. "Could you be any more vague?" she asked. "No wonder you're only getting messages from creeps and going on dates with guys who aren't compatible with you." She told me I needed to go deeper in my profile, I needed to expose a more authentic picture of myself if I wanted to attract the kind of men who I was compatible with.

I had to take a real moment to reconsider the question, *Who am I?* The time had come to stop hiding behind vague and ambiguous answers and instead face the necessary questions: How do I see myself? How do I want to be seen? What sort of man do I want to attract?

I beefed up my interests and expanded my "About Me" sections from guarded bulletpoints to fully formed paragraphs. I answered the compatibility questions and I even took Robert's advice and added more pictures of me engaging in fun activities and making *somewhat* sultry faces.

I called Granny and tried to impart some of my friends' positive dating vibes. As usual, she was a tough cookie to crack. By seventy-five, you think you have the answers to questions. You think you'll know yourself, but the scary truth is, the learning process never ends. Life is like a hike, there will always be another mountain to climb. It was not going to be easy getting Granny to scale the next hill or to even admit that there was a hill out there that she hadn't climbed.

She didn't feel it was necessary to take a second pass at her profile, but I sneakily added some details for her that I suspected would attract men who were more her speed. Along with her love of biscotti and cappuccino, I added some of the hot spots she's traveled to and that she was capable of driving at night (a perk in the senior world). I also included a picture of her with my mom, sisters, and me to give her profile lurkers a better idea of the line of ladies she produced.

# Junk in the Trunk

WITH MY NEWLY HONED profile I was getting fewer messages from topless creeps and corporate weirdos. When Eric—an 89 percent match who worked as a graphic designer and shared my affinity for *Mad Men*—messaged me, I was psyched. I wasn't getting my hopes up for him to be a home run, but I had a good feeling about him.

In an attempt to look sexy for our date, I ended up packing something extra along for the ride. It wasn't intentional; I set out to look casual/cool. I wasn't going to flaunt my bare boobs around like I did for the dating junkie. I wish I could say it was because I had learned my lesson, but truthfully, autumn was upon us and I needed more coverage. As I was getting dressed I spotted a pair of padded underwear in my drawer. A weird thing to have, I totally agree.

The previous winter I was in Puerto Rico with some friends, one of the many trips I took while avoiding the devastation of my Charlie breakup. In PR we kept seeing commercials for Booty Pop, a pair of underwear that operates like a padded bra for your butt. "Go from flat to fab in a pop," they advertised. "Wanna look like J.Lo? No problem, Booty Pop."

Although I like my body, I've always wanted a little extra junk in the trunk. Don't judge me.

Yearning to give me everything I wanted, my loving friends ordered me a pair for my birthday as a joke. Or at least I think it was a joke . . .

As I was getting ready for my date with Eric I spotted the Booty Pop that had been hidden away for months. I slid them on underneath a pair of black stretchy jeans and examined my rump in the mirror. *Oh yes,* I thought, nodding and doing some ga-dunk-a-dunk moves. Then, *Oh no*—it was inappropriate and weird and I couldn't possibly leave the house in them . . . Or could I?

I arrived at the charming West Village cocktail bar of Eric's choice and propped myself up on the barstool. Because of the added oomph in my pants, I was an extra inch or two higher than normal.

Eric strolled into the bar and came in for a kiss on the cheek; balancing on my butt pads, I leaned into him. I was pleased by his scruffy look and feel. Although he lived in Jersey City, he had a very Williamsburg look to him. Beard, glasses, flannel. I was digging it.

Eric's messages interested me because he managed to be thoughtful, intellectual, and funny all at once. That's a tough feat for an OkCupid message, but he did it. In person, he started out with the common nerves that most of us carry on an OkCupid date . . . most of us, except those of us with Booty Pop who have a boost of ego and ass.

When I sensed his shyness, I went into overdrive, asking him questions, asking myself questions, answering for both of us. I realized I was coming off crazy but I couldn't stop the train. I started telling him about my Chinese animal sign. I don't know anything about the Chinese calendar except that

I'm a rabbit and it happened to be the year of the rabbit, but that didn't stop me from bullshitting my way through a whole character profile of the animal. We whipped out our phones and googled to find out Eric was a dog. I asked which dog Eric felt he could most relate to. A boxer? A collie? An English springer spaniel? He settled on a hound dog.

According to the Chinese zodiac, dogs and rabbits are not compatible, but I had hope for the hound dog and me. After ordering a second round of fancy muddled cocktails, we both began to ease up. By ease up, I mean he began to talk and I began to make shit up. He told me about a Proust book he was reading. "I love Proust," I lied. I remember trying to read Proust in college and giving up to watch reality TV instead.

He nodded. "What's your favorite of his books?"

I took a large gulp of my drink, some of the mint catching in my teeth. "Oh, it's hard to choose. All of them, I guess."

He was a smart guy; I'm sure he read through my lies. To change the subject I nodded at the small TV on mute above the bar where a basketball game was playing. "You play any sports?"

"I used to play baseball in high school, but now I'm more of a spectator. Do you like baseball?" he asked.

"Totally," I said with way too much enthusiasm. He looked so pleased by my response I couldn't hold back. "I go all the time. I had season tickets last year." I went *once* last season and I had *a* ticket. I know nothing about baseball but I do know a lot about beer, foam fingers, cotton candy, and making sexy faces when you get on the Jumbotron.

"No way! That's great. We could go to a game together sometime." He smiled at me so sweetly all I could do was nod and bring my fist out for him to bump it like a bro. He shyly crumpled his hand into a ball and tapped mine. I made a low *woof* sound; he looked at me confused and uncomfortable.

"Get it? Hound dogs?" I blushed.

He nodded and forced a smile so I wouldn't feel so lame.

When we got up to leave, I started to feel self-conscious about my butt. Could he tell I was wearing Booty Pop? Had it shifted while I was sitting? Did I look like a Kardashian? Or, more likely, did it look like I was wearing a diaper? As we walked down the block I did a bit of a sideways sashay to avoid my bottom being in his view.

Despite my weirdness, Eric asked for my number and said he'd like to see me again. When we exchanged digits, I began putting him in my phone as "Eric OkCupid." Everyone I meet gets a label next to their name—I'm horrible at names, it's a memory thing. Jessica Summer Camp, Lisa Work, Brad Don't Pick Up, etc. . . . Eric saw his label and requested I change it to "Eric Hound Dog." Slick move.

We did a brief good-bye hug, then I crossed the street. I thought he was taking a turn and he must have thought I was jumping into a cab, but instead we both continued walking down the block on opposite sides of the street. I did a stiff wave and we both laughed at how awkward it was. He turned on the next corner and yelled, "Bye, Kayli OkCupid."

I yelled back, "Bye, Robert OkCupid," then we both froze. This was not Robert, this was Eric. Ugh! I was so preoccupied with concealing my tush and the whole name-saving game got me mixed up.

His mouth formed a tight-lipped smile. From down the block he yelled back, "It's Eric, Eric Hound Dog," then kept walking.

"I'm sorry," I screamed. "That was embarrassing, I know your name, I swear!" I was on a busy corner of Bleecker Street.

An old man looked at me and gave a disapproving shake of the head. I'm not sure if it was from eavesdropping on my flub or noticing the uneven pads in my pants. Either way I walked the rest of the way home cringing at my blunder and cursing my stupid Booty Pop.

Granny had a good giggle when I recounted my date with Eric Hound Dog. She offered some encouraging words: "He thinks you're nuts. I've got no doubt. Between your weird ass pads, your zodiac jabber, then you call him the wrong name?" She burst out in more laughter. "I'm embarrassed just thinking about it. He probably thought you were drugged. I'm your blood and I think you may have lost it."

I wasn't drugged, I hadn't lost it, but it's undeniable that I was weird. Needless to say I never heard from Eric again. "You're on the case of this lawyer fellow for lying about his interests in travel, the artist for maybe not really being an artist, you're on my bones for rounding my age down, meanwhile you're stuffing your ass and talking about star signs like a gypsy?" she asked.

"Hey, hey, hey—" I began.

"It's a two-way street, kid. If you want them to be real with you, you have to hold up your end of the bargain. The same rules apply on both sides." Oh, my wise sage. In order for online dating, or any dating for that matter, to work, everyone needs to be honest with themselves and their dates. Bottom line, at some point or another the jig will be up and your true self will come out.

"I'm weird," I huffed.

"Kid, you're terrific. Maybe a little weird, but definitely terrific. Only a fool wouldn't love the real you."

# Southern Comfort

B Y OCTOBER THE CHILL of fall was sinking in and so was my intolerance for the one-hit wonders I had been encountering on the web. Everyone knows that being single and sexy in the city works best in the summer. Fall is for getting cozy over hot toddies and frisky under flannels. I needed to get serious about finding a blanket buddy. Brad looked like he could be the man for job.

Brad messaged me over Columbus Day weekend. He had just moved to the city from Georgia and his profile was full of pictures of him in exotic locations and adventurous situations. Being that he was a newbie to the city and fresh blood on the site, I figured there was a chance he was an untapped catch. If he had just moved to New York he probably wasn't online dating because he was socially awkward, pervy, or a player (like a large population of male online daters I'd encountered). He was online because he didn't know anyone and wanted to connect with new people. Who was I to deny him that?

He didn't send a message with winking smiley faces or lazy mispellings like the popular "wat's up wit u sweeti?" He sent a

quote by Jonathan Franzen, one of the authors I had listed in
my "Favorites" section. It was a good way of proving that he
was literate and that we shared a common interest. Based off
his profile things were looking good, but you never know until you meet someone face-to-face.

I wanted to get together, but at first our schedules weren't
lining up. A few weeks had passed in our correspondence
when he wrote, "I guess you grew chicken feet. No biggie,
life gives you soup and alley ways, but rarely free beer." It was
a weird message, but I like weird. I also like sayings and his
soup and beer one was floating well with me.

Robert Fulghum wrote, "We are all a little weird. And
life's a little weird. And when we find someone whose weirdness is compatible with ours, we join up with them and fall in
mutually satisfying weirdness—and call it love—true love."
Would Brad's weirdness complement my own?

We set a date the following day to grab a drink at the
Ace, an ultra hip bar located in the swanky Midtown establishment packed with ultracool clientele. When I spotted
him nervously pacing on the sidewalk, I was pleased to see
he was even better looking than his photos let on. He was a
redhead. Before you start discriminating against the gingers,
think Ewan McGregor with a wilderness edge. Now make a
low growling sound under your breath. Yup, he was like that.

He picked the place, so I assumed he knew what the scene
was like. But, when we walked into the crowd of after-work,
suit-wearing yuppies, my guy in his fleece and hiking boots
looked like he was sorely out of place. "Sixteen dollars for two
beers?" he yelled with a southern drawl over the "so hot right
now" crowd to the bartender. He wasn't trying to be rude or
sarcastic, he was honestly just mystified by New York prices.

Although he may have been startled by the cost of the

drinks, he would under no circumstances let me pay for them. And even though he was new to New York, he tipped the bartender a full 20 percent and gave her a charming southern smile as she handed us our eight-dollar beers. I exhaled, and briefly celebrated in my head the discovery that Brad had manners *and* the means to pay for drinks. I led him to a couch past the bar. I hoped his warm grin and alluring profile were promising signs for his personality.

Once we got comfortable, I tried to crack the southern beast. He liked travel. Who doesn't? He was starting a new job. I could have guessed that. Based off his outdoorsman woodsy attire, I took him for a tree-hugging, dog-petting, granola-crunching type. It was hard to know for sure. He was every bit the stoic southern man, a master of the concise answer and glazed-over gaze. I tried my hardest to encourage some basic conversation, but it was like pulling teeth getting him to open up.

I wasn't sure if his dazed-out look was from his discomfort in the too hip environment, his disinterest in me, or some really strong weed. I hoped for the latter, but as we finished our beers, I decided to assume the worst: he wasn't feeling me. I was ready to cut my losses when he finally spoke up. Rubbing his temples, he apologized, telling me about his crazy week at work. He was totally exhausted and having trouble focusing. He suggested we do dinner later in the week.

I thought he might be looking for a way to blow me off. I have definitely used the "let's catch up next time" excuse before. Like he wrote, "No biggie, life gives you soup and alleyways . . . ," but to my surprise, he texted an hour after our date to set up plans.

I was on the fence about a second date, but then I thought back to Granny's feelings about Mike, an OkCupider I got drinks with a few weeks prior. I knew Mike was the type of guy that Granny would consider to be a great candidate for grandson-in-law. I could picture bringing him home for Thanksgiving and Granny force-feeding him shrimp cocktail and piles of dry turkey while he smiled and politely asked for more.

Mike was a nice Jewish boy from Brooklyn. I've dated Jews before, typically out of coincidence rather than preference. It makes no difference to me, but I know that any man who knows what gefilte fish is or has ever asked the four questions would score some serious points in Granny's book.

He was a total gentleman. The guy lived deep in Brooklyn, but he chose Marshall Stack, a low-key bar in my Lower East Side neighborhood, to meet up. I once asked my sister what stuck out about her boyfriend on their first date; she mentioned his considerate gesture of picking a place that was convenient for her.

I guess it takes more than a chivalrous deed to get me hot. Sadly, I just didn't feel any connection with him. He was like plain turkey on white bread. No condiments.

Mike had a good job as a consultant; he was close with his family, worked hard, was good looking, and moderately funny. He was straight edge until college, no drinking or smoking until age twenty, a parent's dream. I, on the other hand, spent my high school years living out a PG-13 version of *Girls Gone Wild* in South Florida.

On paper (or a computer screen), Mike was a solid catch, but I wasn't feeling it. There was zero spark. I'm sure many gals around town would have been tickled to spend an evening with the well-mannered lad, but he wasn't for me. After a few drinks and chitchat about first class versus coach and whether Starbucks coffee was overrated, I told him I had an early morning and had to get home.

Being the nice guy that he was, he offered to walk me back to my apartment. Being the cynic that I am, my first thoughts were: a) he's going to try to come upstairs to get down; b) he wants my address to stalk me; and c) he is going to murder me. None of that happened (at least not yet).

When we got to my door, he hugged me (perhaps lingering for a little too long) and said good night, then we parted ways. For the record, I am not opposed to a nice guy; it's just that I won't settle for plain turkey. I want pickles, tomatoes, olives, banana peppers, pepper jack cheese, and some spicy mustard on my sandwich.

When I told Granny about Michael, she reacted exactly as I had expected. "If you find one thing about him interesting, give him a second chance."

"But I wasn't attracted to him," I whined.

"You don't have to go to bed with him," she insisted. "Maybe you'll find something intriguing. Go to dinner with him, sit around, eat your dinner. If you don't like what you hear, then leave. At least you get a free dinner."

She had a point. "I do like free dinners."

"Just sit, have dinner, chat, whatever you call it. What do you call it when you're twenty-four?" she asked.

"We call it dinner too."

"You never know where something is going to lead," she said. I didn't take her advice with Mike, but I felt like it was time for me to step it up, give Granny some credit, and go for a second date. There were a lot of things I could like about Brad the southern gent. He may have given me some soup, but I decided to go back for seconds.

"He didn't give you soup," Granny corrected. "He is certainly not soup. Hot water? Maybe. Soup? Nope, no way." I gave an affirmative grunt to encourage her on. "Go on a second date though; you have to see if he can bring it to a boil, throw some carrots and noodles in, maybe even a little spice."

I was excited for take two with Brad and pumped for Momofuku, the hip Asian restaurant he picked for our date. For someone fresh in the big city, the guy knew how to pick a spot. Kudos to him and *New York Magazine*.

Again, I spotted him outside wearing the same fleece, hiking boots, and fish-out-of-water expression from our previous date. I looked down at my tiny dress, fur vest, and ridiculous heels. I'm not sure why I went for an upscale-escort-themed look. You should never judge a book by its cover, but if you did, you wouldn't stock me and Brad anywhere near each other on the bookstore shelves.

I went in for my standard double-cheek kiss/hug/handshake hello. As we settled in, Brad mentioned that he had spent some time in Asia. He took the reins in ordering, a manly move that I adore.

When I asked him about his time in Asia he said, "Yeah, it was cool." When I pressed for more details he gave me the same distant gaze from our last date and chose to elaborate by saying, "There was a lot to see. It was fun."

*Okay,* I thought. *Back to me.* I told him about my afternoon at the Russian and Turkish Baths in the East Village, where they have somewhat seedy but relaxing steam rooms and saunas, and gigantic Russian men who will whip you with eucalyptus leaves if you want. (Who wouldn't want that?)

"I spent some time is Russia," he began. "I actually became really good friends with the head of the Russian mafia in the area I was living in." My eyes lit up. Yes! Scandal! I was ready for the juice. "He had a sauna/steam room situation in his house where he'd have parties every Saturday night."

I did a mini fist pump under the table. I *knew* my future boyfriend would be filled with culturally exciting tales. I nodded encouragingly, awaiting gritty details about prostitutes, drug rings, and pet dragons wearing sapphire necklaces. "What were the parties like? How crazy did they get?"

He shrugged. "It was pretty chill. We just hung out and steamed and talked."

I had better Russian mafia stories from Coney Island than he had from the motherland. I chugged on through dinner, trying to get him to open up. The food was crazy hot, but the conversation was bland. He kept dropping bombs of almost interesting stories but then couldn't follow through with any real content or enthusiasm. He was a smart and interesting man but definitely more toned down and serious than I could see myself being with. I wanted a man to entertain, inspire, and excite me (in and out of the bedroom). Brad didn't seem cut out for the job.

He paid like the polite guy that he was, then we walked out to the street to say our good-byes. He leaned in — I thought he was going to kiss me and I wouldn't have stopped him, but he didn't. He just gave me a big ole bear hug and a pat on the back. I didn't know if it was the southern gentleman in him or if the connection truly wasn't there, but after I got home he texted to tell me he had a great time and wanted to know when we could get together next. I didn't want more hot water; I needed a heartier soup.

Granny suspected that Brad wasn't who he said he was. "Is he for real? Or is he telling stories?" she pried like a private eye.

"On paper he's very interesting, but in real life he doesn't have much to say," I told her, trying to shake off any feelings of disappointment.

"Yeah, well, on paper he can be very interesting because he can select to be creative. He can write what he wants and it doesn't have to be his real life," she said, sounding like a true online dating pro. "It's not typical male—an interesting man wants to let you know that he's an interesting man."

That's especially true for men of her age. They've lived a life and want you to know just how exciting it was. "How does he show you he's interesting? Conversationally or sexually," she affirmed.

"He was interesting but I wasn't interested."

"Well, he just met you, so he's gotta start with conversation and he's gotta be interesting to keep you interested. But this one, he sounds like a deadhead."

He was weird, I am weird, but we didn't share a mutual weirdness. Falling for someone, at any age, should be easy and unavoidable—when it feels forced you're doing something wrong. I wasn't going to settle or jump into something just because I was ready for a partner. I learned that lesson the hard way with Tom.

Tom was a friend who I slept with, plain and simple. Or at least I wish it could have been plain and simple, but it never is when you fuck your friends. Tom had been an incredible support to me during my breakup. He'd take me to dinner, let me cry on his couch, get coffee and stroll with me as I shamefully told him about the losers I was sleeping with in my rebound stage. He patiently listened, gave advice, and made me laugh.

Sometimes when he was drunk he'd tell me how much he liked me, but we were friends so I just laughed it off, never bringing it up in our sober moments. Poor Tom. I took advantage of his feelings and confused our friendship in a desperate moment.

I blame Jenna Jones. I let my ego get the better of me and in a desperate attempt to kick-start my relationship status, I racked my mental man list for a quality potential mate, but the only good guy who came to mind was Tom.

Although I had never felt sexually attracted to him, I hoped it was something that I could build through my huge attraction to him as a person. I spent a week chasing him, trying my best to exude my most flirtatious self. I'd flip my hair, bat my eyelashes, and wiggle my cleavage in his face . . . but he didn't lay a finger on me.

I was left with only one option: full-on seduction. I know how that sounds, and trust me, in real life it was even more embarrassing. After a barbecue at my place all my friends left but Tom lingered. We were full of hot dogs and beer when I suggested watching a movie. Lying on my bed in front of my laptop, drunk and irrational thoughts swirled through my head. I waited, dying for him to make a move, but he didn't. I decided to take matters into my own hands. I straddled the poor guy and stuck my tongue down his throat. (You may notice a theme of me forcing myself on men . . . I swear it doesn't happen as often as it seems.) He tried to stop me, which only fueled my desire.

"We're friends, this will change everything," he warned.

I was a fool. I was relentless. I was on a mission, which I should have never aimed to accomplish. We "dated" for a month. That's the thing with dating friends: you know each

other so well that emotions escalate far too quickly. After one
*very* drunk incident where Tom tickled my belly button, mis-
taking it for my *vagina*, I had to call it quits. We were not
compatible beyond friendship. I loved being around him,
and I so badly wanted there to be a romantic spark but there
wasn't. You can't create or deny chemistry.

Granny was in a marriage where they faked it for more
than two *decades*. "We had a big problem: I was never physically attracted to him *at all*," she said. "It wasn't the same for
him. You must have sexual chemistry. He was always chasing
me and I was always running away." She ran right into the
arms of another man.

Although her affair with Ira was adulterous and all, there
was no denying that they had the kind of chemistry that rat-
tles your soul. The type that inspires poets, starts wars, and
makes you want to shave your legs every day. Their spark was
so strong it was enough for her to risk it all and cling to for a
lifetime. She tried to end it several times—she was a married
woman after all—but it was impossible. They were addicted
to each other.

"It would get too complicated and I couldn't stand it anymore. I'd literally begin to have a nervous breakdown trying
to live two lives so I'd end it," she confessed. "But we couldn't
be apart, no matter what we couldn't be apart." At one point,
fifteen years into their affair, she called it off and managed
to avoid him for months. Her plan was going well until her
husband decided they should move. He picked a building in
Edgewater, New Jersey. The building next door was Ira's.

"I waited a week of living there until one day I couldn't
take it and I slowly drove past his building entrance. I was dying to catch a glimpse of him," she admitted. "The instant I

walked into my apartment the phone rang. I picked it up and it was him."

"How'd he get your number?" I asked.

"When you want to get to someone, you get to them." Oh, he got to her, all right. But now it was finally over. Their history and spark had fizzled out, and all she was left with was the regret for not trying harder to make it work when it could have and for wasting decades on regret in her singledom after it was over.

I gave Granny the advice she had been giving me: Date some men who fit your criteria and date some who don't. She needed to let go of her strict ideals.

She brought up Todd, a fella she had been sharing flirtatious messages with. Based off his profile, the guy sounded like a total catch. He was retired from NASA. An astronaut! The man worked on Apollo, a bit of information that I thought sexy but Granny found wholly intimidating. "This is a kind of smart that isn't in my world, this is different smart," she said.

"So you'd rather play it cool and be alone in your comfort zone?" I pushed her. She had been preaching to me to date men in different fields; it was time for her to take a dose of her own medicine.

"Jesus," she huffed. "I'm going out with him tonight, chill your beans."

Four hours later my phone rang. Granny was on the other line. "I'm gonna start from the end: he's a very nice man."

I breathed a premature sigh of relief.

"A very nice man, but he looks like a walrus."

"What?" I asked.

She began to explain to me what a walrus is. "You know, a large wooly sea mammal? Cousin to the seal? This guy was a walrus. Big chest and belly, silver facial hair like whiskers, and on top of it he was wearing stripes. Stripes that went the *wrong* way."

You would think that once you pass your seventies looks and fashion wouldn't be important, but apparently that's not the case.

They met up at Dunkin' Donuts for coffee, but once he took a look at the little hotcake that is my granny he said, "I don't want just coffee with you. I wanna take you somewhere to have a whole meal."

On the way to the restaurant she asked where he lived. "I'm in a mobile," he said.

"Mogul?" she asked.

"Mobile," he repeated.

This exchange went on a few too many times until Granny said, "The only moguls I know are on a ski slope and I don't know any of those in South Florida."

"No, I got myself a double-wide," he said.

It sounded like the rest of the night's conversation was full of little misunderstandings and inabilities to relate.

He took her to a restaurant in my hometown, Jupiter, called the Thirsty Turtle, known for its hot wings and rowdy teenage crowd. "I was eating dinner at a quarter after five," she snarled. "I've never had dinner so early in my life. I've had lunches that started later. Only old people eat dinner before six," she said without any intended irony.

Granny alerted my mom, who lives around the corner from Thirsty Turtle, to her whereabouts. My mother then proceeded to conduct a covert operation to spy on the date. Based off my mom's account, it sounded like a ridiculous scene: there was a window and some not-so-discreet waving and awkward neck-jerking gestures.

"Overall, how was it? A fun night?" I asked.

"Kid, my night was over before seven. It was a pleasant *evening.* Like I said, he's a nice man, but we move at different speeds."

We can't help who we love, the type of people that attract us, or the clowns who repel us. Even though Granny wasn't swooning for the Walrus, a date with a walrus is better than no date at all.

# Penny-Pinchers

I MIGHT BE A SHITTY granddaughter. Is it wrong to force your granny to go on a date against her will? Besides my own selfish wishes to be entertained by her tales, I swear I thought it would be nice for her to keep the dating momentum strong. When Tim, Granny's online dating virginity snatcher, invited her out for a second outing, I was all for it. She was the one pushing me to give second chances; why shouldn't the same rules apply to her?

He sent an email inviting Granny for dinner, adding, "You said that next time was your treat. Think I'll accept that . . . P.S. Of course I'll pay for drinks."

She wasn't taking the bait. "He's a self-involved schmuck. There is no way in hell I'm taking him out to dinner."

"He's just being cheeky," I argued. I didn't think there was even a chance he'd let her pay. He's an old retired fellow with a boat and a large home. I assumed he'd have the funds or at least the gentlemanly manners to treat a classy older lady to a meal, especially since he was the one to ask her out.

"He's short and angsty—you know how short men have that complex," she whined.

"I'm familiar with the complex, but I won't accept it as a viable excuse."

"You wouldn't go out with a man that's five-four."

"You're right, but I am seven inches taller than you."

"He talks nonstop."

"So do you." We went back and forth until she finally caved and agreed to go for round two with Tim.

They went to an upscale restaurant on the water. A spot Tim had chosen. As they looked over their menus, they heard popping sounds in the distance. "Must be fireworks," Granny casually remarked.

He grunted and quickly dismissed her. "I know a pistol when I hear one."

When the waitress came by to apologize for the loud firecrackers, Tim pretended to be busy with his napkin. According to Granny, he completely monopolized the conversation, as she promised he would. "He didn't remember a goddamn thing about me. He didn't remember if I had a son or a daughter or that I was from New York," she complained. "This was our second date. I'd like to blame it on his old age but the truth is he's just a self-involved bastard." Granny is not one to let bad behavior slide.

"Did you call him out on it?"

"I *casually* told him that I'd heard some men were online dating to find a *nurse* or a *purse*." Granny was beginning to develop a theory on older men's intentions in online dating. A nurse-seeker is someone who is looking for a lady to take care of him; a purse-seeker is looking for a lady to support him.

"What did he say?"

"The old fart got offended and said he has never heard

such a thing." She giggled, pleased with herself for causing him to stir. "Bullshit, he's looking for both."

"Maybe he was having a bad day," I suggested, trying my hardest to play devil's advocate.

"No, kid, it's just the way he is. Old people are comfortable enough to put themselves out there the way they are. For better or, in Tim's case, worse."

"Did he let you pay?" I asked.

She inhaled deeply, which is never a good Granny sign. "As soon as the bill came he pushed it in front of me." She gave a dramatic pause for emphasis. "Let me give you our order"—she was practically growling—"I had a piece of cod and a glass of wine. He had a salad, two glasses of wine, crab legs, *and* a coffee."

Of course Granny, being the penny-pincher that she is, remembered the cost of every item. "My fish? Thirteen dollars. His *meal,*" she said, stretching out the vowels, "it was *forty-eight dollars.*" She put eighteen dollars on the table, then went to the bathroom where she contemplated calling a cab or my mother to come pick her up. "I wasn't far from home. I thought it would have been cheaper to take a cab than pay for his dinner."

When she returned to the table he rudely stated, "You owe more."

"*What* is more?" she asked.

He pushed the check in front of her again. She reluctantly took out more bills. This was not the sort of traditional date demeanor Granny, at seventy-five, was used to.

"Apparently that's the way it is now," she said to me as if she were discovering a new tip in a magazine. Her tone shifted from bitter disbelief to amicable understanding. "If a man takes you to dinner once or twice, then you have to take him to dinner. That's what's happening these days."

"Ugh, *these* days," I commiserated.

"If he were a gentleman that wanted to continue things, he would have said, 'You get it next time.' That repertoire would have continued as a tactic for him to get to spend more time with me." She sounded almost upbeat at her revelation. "He played it all wrong." I had to agree; the jerk should have paid for his own freaking crab legs.

When he dropped her off at her home she said good-bye. "I meant it, kid. *Good-bye.* That's it. Never again."

"Adios."

"The *positive* thing," she began (and boy, was I glad to hear there was an upside), "it's nice to know it's a learning experience even at seventy-*whatever.* I'm still learning."

It's the twenty-first century and I'm a moneymaking gal. I have no problem picking up the check or at least paying my half of the bill, but to me that feels like a modern development that shouldn't apply to a date between two people in their seventies. I'm not the type to seek a sugar daddy or a man to support me in any financial way (although I am accepting presents and if you want to pay off my college loans I won't stop you). Thrifty is one thing, cheap is another. I love a deal. I'm a total bargain hunter. Two-dollar tacos, happy hours, secondhand stores, and Living Social are all things I can get down with. Cheap men are not.

After Granny's date I was extra sensitive to the penny-pinching breed, which might help to explain why I had no patience for James, a Noah Wyle look-alike and ruthless man-child. He chose Temple Bar, a dark and intimate spot in SoHo that he found on Yelp for our date. James had lived in the city for close to ten years, so it seemed a little odd that he needed to use Yelp to find a bar, but I decided to consider it thoughtful that he was doing some research.

Cocktails were around fourteen dollars. That's definitely not a bargain, but in New York it's not uncommon. Since James had bragged about looking up the establishment online, I assumed he'd have an idea of how much it would cost.

Throughout our snoozy conversation James brought up more than once that he often eats cereal for dinner. He's eight years out of college. I should have read this as a warning sign. When the check came it was twenty-nine dollars. He looked at it like it was a speeding ticket and at our waitress (who had been incredibly friendly and accommodating) like she was the offending officer.

When I offered to pay for my half he affected his best macho tone and insisted on paying. He handed the waitress two twenties. She came back with two fives and a one, eleven dollars. James made a snide laugh when he saw the change. "Look, look what this waitress is trying to tell me."

I looked at the money, failing to see any cryptic message.

"She brought back two fives and a one because she's saying the tip should be five dollars. No way," he said, grabbing the two fives and leaving our poor waitress a one-dollar tip.

I had worked in the service industry for too long to stand for such shitty behavior. I was lucky to cocktail at a nightclub where the gratuity is automatically included, but not all waitresses are so fortunate. Servers don't make a salary; tips are how they pay their bills. One dollar can't even buy you a pack of gum in the city.

I gave him a disapproving look as I reached for my wallet

to put my own money in. "It's cool, let me pay for my drink," I insisted.

"No," he said defensively. "Tell me what you would do."

"Drop the cash," I instructed. Then I snatched the five up and handed it back to him, leaving six dollars on the table. "That's twenty percent. This is New York, that's what you do."

"But then the waitress's plan worked," he said like a child defeated in a game.

"I'm *pretty* sure there was no plan on her part. She was just doing her job."

Needless to say, it was an awkward end to the date. Knowing how much Granny hates a tightwad, I thought she'd be more on board with me when I told her about the interaction.

She agreed I shouldn't see James again but said, "Don't criticize, kid, no one likes to be criticized."

"But I can't stand for that."

"So it makes it better if you're rude back to him?"

"Maybe . . ." I tried to defend myself.

"He'd get the message just as easily if you never went out with him again."

Granny led by example. She wiped her hands of Tim and came out on top without engaging in any argumentative banter. Surprisingly, I liked her advice. It was a classy alternative to my bitchy retort.

# Club Rats

"**Y**OU HAVE TO PUT YOURSELF out there more — in the *real* world." After months of watching her second favorite granddaughter fail at finding love on the web, Granny gave me some old-school advice. "Stop limiting yourself. These online guys are fine and good, but you got the goods, go out there and work 'em."

I had tried and bombed at that. It was no secret that after Charlie I was incapable of, or perhaps intentionally failing at, choosing the right guys in real life. I was either diving into quasi-relationships out of comfort or jumping into bed with bozos for distraction, which was what got us on the dating sites in the first place.

"Where do you suppose I put my *goods* to work?"

"A hotel dance," she said without an ounce of sarcasm.

"What is a hotel dance?"

"When I was a girl, and that was a *hundred* years ago," she began with a cheeky tone, "dances were a *really* big deal. Hotel dances were the *real* big deal. That's where I met your grandfather, the very first time I went, at the Vanderbilt Hotel."

"So I should go to hotel dances?" I joked.

"Yes," she answered definitively.

"There are no hotel dances. That doesn't exist."

She wasn't listening; she had an idea and she wouldn't shut up until she made sure I heard it. "Find a girlfriend and go out to one. Get dressed up, you know in something flattering. Maybe even a little number with a high hemline, show off those legs of yours. Fix yourself up and hit the hotel dances," she instructed.

"Today's equivalent to a hotel dance is a nightclub."

"A nightclub? It wasn't a nightclub, it was a hotel dance."

"Exactly, I *work* at a modern-day hotel dance."

"No, no, no, I'm talking about a live band, you know?"

"There are DJs now."

"No, it's different," she insisted. "At hotel dances the men would look over the women—"

"Trust me the men still look over the women."

She persisted. "In your grandfather's case he was with a female friend. He said to her, 'Go over and talk to her and see what she's like.' She obviously told him I was a good one because he came over and asked me to dance." She was giddy recounting the story. "At the time he was doing a *really* hot cha-cha-cha. With a hop and a skip and a jump. And I said, 'What is *that*? Where are you from? Brooklyn?'" She cracked herself up. Being able to distinguish what borough someone was from based on his cha-cha style is a nostalgic idea, similar to today's fist pump alluding to a Long Island origin.

"No one does the cha-cha anymore and no man who is boyfriend material would be in a nightclub, hotel dance, whatever you want to call it."

As a cocktail waitress I get hit on a lot. It's just the way it works. The waitress is an easy target for a man to practice his game on. I think it's fair to assume that most girls working in nightlife are used to lewd advances, mastering the "back away, I'm unapproachable" glare, and saying things like, "Sorry, I have a boyfriend," when they don't.

When I was in middle school my older sister worked in an ice cream shop. I was insanely jealous. She could eat as much chocolate chip cookie dough as her heart desired. After a few months of scooping cones she confessed, "I like ice cream, but when you're around it all the time you just don't feel like eating it. It's too much. The smell of it is unappetizing."

Essentially, I worked in a man shop. I get how my sister must have felt about ice cream. It's not that I was less attracted to men, it's that I was more suspicious of them. I've seen countless fellas with bands on their fingers and tequila on their breath shamelessly try to score with giggly airhead models, or get drunk and turn from a sweet businessman into total perv. Call it cynical, call it bitchy, call it jaded . . . whatever you call it, my working environment was definitely taking a toll on my view of men.

When I became single it was rare for me to even consider going out with guys I met in the club. That's not to say that I didn't have my occasional sexual fix (ugh, yes, I know I attacked an Argentinean scenester), but those guys were never the type of men that I'd actually qualify as a real partner. That was part of the appeal of online dating in the first place; I was going to meet guys from different circles who would see me as a dating prospect and not just the floozy slinging the booze. My plan for avoiding club rats was going well until I met Nate.

Nate, an Australian built like a professional athlete with

chiseled cheekbones that could inspire a Disney prince, approached me at work in late fall. Measuring in at six-seven—count it out: that is seventy-nine inches of man—he was hard to miss standing at the bar. I rarely go for men who are better looking than me or ones who I meet in the club, so I did my best to avoid paying him any attention.

Despite my efforts at being standoffish, I kept running into him throughout the night as I scrambled through the room delivering bottles and death stares to patrons. I assumed our run-ins were just coincidence until he stuck his head in the server station and asked, "When are you going to talk me?"

I was ready to give him one of my scathing responses, but when I looked up at his eyes, a soaring foot above my own, he was just too adorable.

"What do you want to talk about?" I asked suspiciously.

"Let's start with your name," he cooed, melting me with his Australian accent.

"Kayli," I squeaked.

"Halley?" he asked, tormenting me with his sexy enunciation.

"Nope, Kayli. Sounds like Halley." He was so handsome he could have called me "Sally Fish Fingers" and I would have let him.

He wooed me with boyhood tales and obscure facts about Halley's Comet. He was like a human encyclopedia—a very handsome and, I suspected, very drunk encyclopedia. It was late, and he was being outrageous and silly, but I had just met him so I let myself believe it was his free spirit.

As he was leaving we swapped phone numbers. "When are you going to call me?" he asked.

"After you call me." I am a lady after all. I looked down at my buzzing phone and saw a number I didn't recognize. He smiled at me. Goddamn, he was charming.

"Okay, I just called you. You have to hit me up next."

I smirked and saved him in my phone as "Nate Hot Aussie," *as if* I would forget the Australian ogre. He leaned in, grabbed my head, and kissed me so passionately I thought my leg might lift up like a cheesy cartoon. He was Casanova and I was a ball of nerves. What the fuck just happened?

It certainly felt like sparks, but I met him in the club, I told myself, I don't go out with guys from there. I let a few days pass but I couldn't get Nate out of my head. It was like when you go shopping and see something you like, but it's expensive and you're not sure if you actually want it, so you wait and, if it's still on your mind days later, you know you need to have it.

He *did* tell me to contact him. It was 2011 and women *can* make the first move, especially if a man *suggests* they do so, I told myself. I debated whether he could be a real prospect, or if I should just write him off as a fun flirt. Then I figured, if I'm messaging with all sorts of men online who are strangers, why not go for one who I've met and know I have some chemistry with.

"You liked him? He was cute? He gave you a smooch? What's the problem?" Granny bullied when I asked her to weigh in.

"It feels too forward to hit up a guy."

"You're the one who keeps telling me to be *more* forward with men," she argued. "Besides what's the difference between messaging a man that you see online and messaging one you meet in real life? Trust your instincts, be spontaneous, stop overanalyzing it."

I grunted. "Yeah, but this guy, I met him in the *club*."

"The guys you meet in the club are creeps—we know this. But you have a good eye, kid. What's the worst that could happen?" That's one of the perks of online dating; it desensitizes you to the idea of going on a date so the pressure to hit up a stranger loses a tinge of its intensity. Going for a drink with someone is just going for a drink with someone; it doesn't have to be the overly analytical experience that it used to be.

I went for it. "What do you know about Halley's Comet?" I texted. It was my attempt at being somewhat witty while hoping to spark up some of the humor from our initial interaction. As soon as the message was sent I put my phone in my bag and didn't look at it, trying to feign disinterest but in reality waiting in a world of suspense.

After an hour of self-enforced aloofness I picked up my phone, elated to see that Nate had texted back. I exhaled, trying to hold back a shit-eating grin as I unlocked my phone. He had been waiting anxiously for my text, I told myself. If he didn't hear from me by the weekend he would have come back to the club to confess that he had full-blown Kayli fever. Every time his phone buzzed his heart skipped a beat, hoping it was me. The wait is over, Nate, I have come for you.

Then I read his message: "I remember seeing it as a kid on my uncle's lawn. *Sorry who is this?*"

It took everything in me not to throw my phone against the wall. I fell for it. I fell for a sleazy club rat!

"It's Kayli, sounds like Halley. You told me all about it." I was seething as I texted. "You then told me to call you. I told you you were too drunk to remember, and here we are."

"Sorry, I must have been really drunk. Facebook me," he wrote.

Oh, hell no. What was up with men using *Facebook* as a

buffer for interaction? In my initial year post-Charlie, I lived in a state of promiscuous mayhem. During this wild streak I had a thrilling sexual rendezvous with a man in France. He had my number and email, but rather than using either to contact me after our Parisian romp, he sent me a goddamn friend request. I know we have to get down with modern technology, but I refuse to allow Facebook as a form of post-coital connection. I never accepted the request, preferring to keep our experience in my head and off the Internet.

Nate had bruised my ego enough for one text conversation. I declined his Facebook offer and didn't text back. I was disappointed in myself for falling for his act in the first place, but just because I took a shot and missed didn't mean I was going to sit on the sidelines and whine about it.

# Don't Stop, Won't Stop

To lift my spirits after "Nate Hot Aussie's" memory loss, I began perusing the dating site How About We. In theory it's a cool site where singles suggest fun dates, then you choose to go out with them based on the itinerary. In practice, I hadn't seen any guys post a date that wasn't cheesy (e.g., *"How about we . . .* walk in the rain in Battery Park then kiss on the street") or lacking creativity (e.g., *"How about we . . .* share a bottle of wine in Little Italy"). Call me crazy, but I wanted someone to suggest: *"How about we . . .* break into the Museum of Natural History and steal some dinosaur bones," or *"How about we . . .* attempt to kidnap a child on the High Line." I wanted danger. I wanted adventure.

*"How about we . . .* go rock climbing at Chelsea Piers?" was the date Justin suggested. Although it didn't involve larceny, I was still into it. Justin claimed to be six feet three inches in his profile. By that point I thought it safe to assume that everyone's height was minus two inches from what their profile stated. I figured that if he was at least six-one there was a chance I'd want to climb *him*. Sweat, muscles, and a harness? Yes, please.

In his profile he wrote, "I'm quiet but not shy." I pondered this a bit.

I read it to Granny, who kindly said, "You're a loudmouth, you're whatever the opposite of quiet is." He could be the yin to my yang.

As I approached the West Side restaurant across from the pier, our planned meeting place to rendezvous, I spotted a tall figure standing in the shadows who looked as though he might *actually* be six-three. I did a tiny excited fist pump. *Oh, hello, Justin.*

After greeting each other, we wandered into the gym together, stumbling out the awkward get-to-know-you chat. It was textbook but unavoidable and beginning to feel easier after so much practice.

In the climbing zone we suited up into some snazzy rock-climbing sneaks and joined a group of other novice climbers all decked out in wilderness wear—sweatproof tops and high-performance pants. Sometimes men can look awkward in gym shorts; Justin definitely did not look awkward in his.

In the lulls between our turns to climb, we had time to chat. I saw what he meant by "quiet but not shy." He was cerebral, quick, but mellow, not a loud, overly chatty type.

We talked about music, art, and theater. (Honestly, I know how cheesy that sounds.) His tastes were more refined and specific than mine. He liked obscure artists from World War II, bands I'd never heard of, and shows I had never seen. When we talked about Halloween, which had been the previous weekend, he told me about going to the opera—I told him about dressing up as Robyn the Swedish pop star.

Although we were very different, we could relate to each

other. His chilled-out vibes were contagious. I felt laid-back and totally captivated by his company. So laid-back that when the combination of the harness and climbing maneuvers contorted my Lycra spandex into a severe camel toe, I only turned a rosy shade of pink rather than a deep beet red.

It's hard to look sexy when you're straddling a rock wall, scraping your limbs, slipping off and then colliding back into the wall, but I tried my best. Because he was so tall and athletic, Justin was the star climber of the group. Watching him hoist himself up the wall gave me great insight to his strength, dexterity, and, um . . . endurance. The other climbers in the class watched him with envy. I proudly shot back a look that said, "Back off, babes, he's with me."

After our climb, we strolled to the train. I was heading downtown, he was going up. We hugged (I was tired of *hugging* men) and made plans to get drinks the following week. I decided if things went well, there was a chance we'd be mounting more than just rock walls.

The next day, as I was superstitiously avoiding looking at my phone, hoping for a message from Justin, "Nate Hot Aussie" struck again. Over text he explained that he had done some significant online lurking, figured out who I was, and wanted to take me out. It was strange that Nate went from not knowing my name to finding online info about me, but as it turns out, he was an expert Google stalker, and these days it's impossible to not have at least one skeleton in your digital closet. The game has changed since 1954, when a man had to send a friend over to get the scoop. This was modern romance where with a few key words and a computer you can find out almost *too* much information.

As far as my ego was concerned, I knew it probably wasn't the best move to go out with a guy who didn't remember meeting or kissing me, but at the same time I was curious about going on a date with a six-foot-seven Australian who I met *offline*, and I didn't want to discount the possibility that he might suffer from temporary amnesia.

When I told Granny, she let me talk in circles and contradict myself nine times about what I was going to do before she piped up. "He's a six-foot-seven Australian, are we really going to pretend that you're *not* going to go out with him? Give me a break."

I couldn't remember the last time a guy I had met *in real life* wanted to take me on a real date. There are hookups and casual hangouts . . . but a date . . . *What the hell?* I thought. I was going out with so many people from OkCupid anyway, why not add one more dude to the list?

We kicked off a flirty text chat, a wit-off if you will, but he was too "busy" to lock down an actual date. In the midst of our banter, I heard back from Justin, who was ready and eager to go for round two. I wasn't going to sit around and wait for Nate. I was excited to see Justin again.

Justin and I had almost nothing in common, which kept things interesting during our rock-climbing outing. Maybe it was his overt display of masculinity. Maybe it was the exercise endorphins my body was releasing. Maybe it was the excitement of something new. Or maybe it was his form-fitting gym shorts. Whatever it was, I hoped to feel it again.

I met him at Barrow Street Ale House in the West Village. He was wearing pants. It was 7 p.m.; we were one beer in when we fell into a lull of conversation. "Wanna do a shot?"

he asked with the enthusiasm of a college sorority girl. I did not want to do a shot. I am no wet noodle, I like to cut loose, but a shot felt like it was forcing the mood. You only start taking shots at 7 p.m. if you are preparing for a rager, getting over a rager, an alcoholic, in college, or planning to puke by 10 p.m. I didn't qualify for any of those things.

"I'm all set, but thanks," I politely declined.

"I usually don't drink beer, I prefer dirty martinis, extra dirty," he said. I laughed, assuming he was joking, because besides the fact that he had chosen an *ale*house for our date, he sounded like Samantha from *Sex in the City*. He stared back at me stoically, unsure of what he said that warranted my giggles.

He kept the same deadpan look when he told me about his hip-hop dance team. He was a tall, white, computer-programming, cardigan-wearing, soft-spoken man, and when he explained the part of rehearsal where they "just groove," I couldn't help but chuckle. The image of a group of gangly white men "grooving" warrants a laugh. Judging by his sober expression, he did not agree.

We moved to Wilfie and Nells, another West Village bar where Justin finally ordered the filthy martini he'd been lusting after. He tongued the olives off his pick like a true diva. In a forced attempt to spice up our conversation he asked me, "What's one secret that no one knows about you?"

I considered. "I killed a hooker in Amsterdam."

He gave me a look that was equal parts horrified and confused. Having different tastes, styles, and hobbies is not a deal breaker, but not being able to make each other laugh is. Justin was an excellent climber, a really nice dude, and I bet a super talented "groover," but we didn't laugh together, and like

Granny felt with her RV man, if I can't laugh with a man there's little chance I will "groove" with him.

"Shots *and* a martini?" was Granny's main question after I debriefed her on the date.

"Yeah."

"Was the shot vodka too or something else?" she asked suspiciously.

"Probably tequila, why?" I was unsure of where her line of questioning was going.

"Oh no, no way. Forget it, no good," she began. "Never trust a man who mixes his alcohol."

Regardless of Justin's boozing patterns, I wasn't feeling it. In fact, all I was feeling was bummed that after almost four months of online dating I had yet to find anyone worthy of a third date. Going out with someone three times is a big thing. After the third date, you usually develop a feeling or two for the other person, or at the very least, enjoy a dry-hump session.

# Speed Bumps

Hi: I am old, and after having been faithfully married
for 45 years, I want to end this life as a playboy. I want to
get as much mileage out of this old body as I can while
everything is still working. I think you are probably looking
for someone for a committed relationship, but I am looking
for a woman for hanky panky until exhaustion sets in!

Best wishes,
Greg

G RANNY'S LUCK WASN'T any better than mine. She
had messages coming in like the one above but very
few amounted to actual dates. We cracked up at
Greg's hornball declaration. "He's being too obvious to be interesting," she said, cackling. "He better put his pants back on
before he hurts himself."

Granny and I weren't the only ones suffering from the dating
blues. Robert, the dating junkie, was facing his own woman
woes. Even though our date was a total dud, New York is a
surprisingly small city. A few months after our awkward date
we ran into each other at a bar in my neighborhood, after

which I caved and accepted his friend request on Facebook. It was clear on both ends that we lacked romantic rapport, but I enjoyed his dark sense of humor and shameless attitude. We were in the same dating trenches, and it was nice to have common ground to gossip about with a like-minded OkCupider.

To swap notes on our dating lives, we planned to meet up at Hotel Delmano, a speakeasy cocktail bar in his neighborhood with fancy drinks and bartenders who wear suspenders and hipster mustaches. Robert was feeling used up and washed out. OkCupid was his bitch. He had slapped it around, tore it apart, and now was left resenting it.

"How often are you using?" I asked

"I'm on about two new dates a week now," he said without an ounce of sarcasm. "In the good days I was doing about five."

He explained his theories of online girls, messaging techniques, and his overall online method of seduction. He was a true master.

"I feel like I've been out with every girl on the site, but I still haven't met any that I want to actually be with."

Partially grossed out but wholly impressed, I suggested that maybe he had gotten all there was to get out of OkCupid. Maybe it was time to move on to greener pastures. I told him about How About We. Since he's a creative guy, I had a feeling he could be a real hit on the site.

I opened the app on my phone and gave him a full-on tutorial. We scoffed at the countless recycled, mundane dates that some of the guys suggested: "*How about we . . .* listen to some tunes at mine and see what happens?" "*How about we . . .* let me treat you like the beautiful lady you are?" "*How about we . . .* drink beer and watch the game?" Let's not all line up at once.

Robert wasn't taking it seriously; he was too busy eyeing a pair of cute French girls sitting at the table beside us, trying to lock eyes with the brunette. "I know that girl," he whispered.

"From where?"

"OkCupid."

I shook my head. This girl was super hot, super French, and (I thought) super out of his league. I didn't believe it was possible for him to recognize a girl in real life that easily from her profile, but he insisted.

"She probably never responded because she's smarter than me and realized that the message you sent was a generic copy and paste," I teased.

He pulled up the OkCupid app on his phone and tried to find her on the site to no avail.

"Why don't you just ask her?" I suggested.

To my surprise he leaned over and said, "Excuse me, I think I know you from somewhere?"

The brunette made a confused smile and shook her head. Then in an *adorable* French accent asked, "Where?"

"I've seen you around . . . on OkCupid," he boldly stated. She turned red, I turned red, Robert may have turned red, but it would have been hard to tell behind his beard.

The online dating gods smiled down on them. She explained that she had been on the site but got off because she hadn't met any good guys. Bringing his cyber confidence into the real world, Robert told her that *he* was a good guy and would love to take her out. Just like that, they swapped numbers, set up a date, and made a connection.

I was impressed not only with his performance and the outcome, but also the bizarre quality of the online dating platform and its ability to act as a connecting force in real life. If anyone could pull it off, it was the dating junkie. I was happy to see Robert's dating libido restored. I was ready for my own twist of fate.

Weeks had passed from the night I met Nate to us locking down a date to meet. The night before we were supposed to get a drink he apologized and told me he'd have to push it to the following night. Under normal circumstances, I would have ended things before they even began. He was clearly a flake, but what the hell. Like Granny said, he was a six-foot-seven Australian. There were worse ways I could spend an evening.

I went into our date with exceptionally low expectations. Without the aid of Google, the guy didn't remember who I was. I pegged him as an obnoxious jock or brain-dead pretty boy, but that's the thing with keeping the bar low: the only way to go is up—a trick of the trade I had picked up and been trying to reiterate to Granny.

I wandered into the Rusty Knot, a nautical-themed bar on the West Side, and saw him sitting by the bar. He smiled in my direction as he stood up and came toward me. My heart skipped a goddamn beat. He was definitely too handsome. "How did you recognize me?" I teased. "I thought you didn't remember anything."

"Come on, I do remember."

"You're just a really good Internet stalker, huh?"

He blushed and nodded, hanging his head from embarrassment. "I'm sorry, I was coming from a friend's birthday party that night. I had way too much to drink and—"

It's good to make men feel a little shitty so they know who is boss. He messed up, he knew it. Now he was lucky enough to get a second chance with me. "It's cool, don't worry about it." I laughed too hard in an attempt to exude some carefree confidence.

He told me he was twenty-eight but was already in the process of opening up a bar in Midtown, an ambitious project for someone of his age. Although I was excited by his drive, I had worked in nightlife for too long to not have a sour impression of the "bar owner" persona. Before I even knew him I was already subconsciously stereotyping him like the corporate lawyer did to me.

While I was busy being judgmental, an older woman approached; she knew Nate from a bar he had previously managed in Australia. His demeanor with her was so kind and considerate I couldn't help but begin to sweeten to him. I tried my best to silence my judgmental thoughts, ease up, and be open.

He wanted to get to know me and asked me several thoughtful questions about my passions and background. I told him about my aspirations to get into TV writing. I was getting tired of wasting all of my time working in the club. I had the itch to pursue a new creative project. Nate listened attentively then stunned me with his knowledge of the business. I was impressed; he was clearly more than just a pretty face.

When he told me about his best friends, his *mom* and *three sisters*, I wanted to pee my pants a little bit. I mean, come on! A man who grew up with a boatload of gals has got to be a unique human being. I have two sisters. Between the three of us we had enough estrogen to kill a horse. Yet the effect it had on Nate seemed to be absurdly positive.

We were having such a good time that he asked if I wanted to get dinner. Realizing that both of us lived on the other side

of town, we strolled in the chilly fall night through the West
Village over to Barrio Chino (the cute Mexican restaurant on
the Lower East Side where I had gone with Robert on our first
date). Chowing down on tacos, we talked until 2 a.m.

Nate made me nervous and excited all at once. It had
been a long time since I felt those genuine emotions. He was
driven, entertaining, and annoyingly charming, and he didn't
even flinch when he tried my jalapeño margarita. When he
walked me home and gave me a kiss, I kissed him back intensely. I knew (hoped) he wouldn't forget it this time.

Four days passed before I heard from him. Although I was
hoping for a message of any kind, I felt more relaxed than I
typically would have after such a rock-star date. I was busy. I
had other dates to go on and men to meet. Sure, I wanted to
go out with him again, but at the same time, you can't put all
your eggs in one basket.

He told me he had to leave the country to renew his visa.
(I considered that he could have made that up . . . It would
be an incredibly tactful way to cut me off.) But he assured
me when he came back, he'd like to go out again. Regardless,
I was grateful for our date for lifting my spirits on the dating
game and reminding me that there is something to be said for
recognizing chemistry in real life.

When I told Granny about Nate she was on the fence just
like me. He had started out lousy but was great in person.
Rather than overthink him or our date, I turned the tables
to get her head back in the game. "You're up, lady," I egged
her on.

She read me a message from Hank, a stocky man with a
furry mustache who painted himself to be a sincere family
man. "He looks like a troll," she teased.

"Enough! Just call him," I insisted.

Like a teenage girl whose mother is forcing her to go to a family reunion, Granny reluctantly agreed. I expected her to call me back ready to talk shit, but when I got a message from her after their chat I couldn't believe what I was hearing. "Two hours I was on the phone, from a quarter to ten to a quarter to twelve," she began. I could hear the disbelief in her voice. "I *like* this man. What do you think of that?" What I thought was that she might have been hitting her Valium a little hard. I've rarely heard her admit to liking *anything* let alone *anyone*.

She started listing their differences. "He is a devout Catholic. He has eight children. I have nothing in common with him . . . But yet I did. He's a New Yorker, six months in New York and six months down here. Unbelievable. Nothing in common. Perfectly charming." She stopped making sentences and started spitting out words. "Amazing. Two hours."

When she snapped out of it, she realized she had taken food out of the freezer prior to their call but had been chatting so long it had already defrosted. "That's how distracted I was!" she hollered. "You should be in shock because I am."

I was, I most definitely was. I knew I should have maintained low expectations, but I couldn't help picturing them in matching pastel-colored sweat suits strolling down the beach, sipping bay breezes and shooting the shit. (Disclaimer: Granny wouldn't be caught dead in pastels or sweat suits unless they were designer, but you get the idea.)

Granny didn't fool around when she was getting ready for this date. She put on her most slimming pantsuit and flattering makeup, and even did her hair. Granny and I, both undeniable grumps, were actually excited for her date with Hank. I imagined there'd be a dramatic embrace, maybe even some watering of the eyes, possibly a slight tap on the behind and a cheeky wink.

As she strutted into the café, she recognized him as the man in the stained hoodie and Bermuda shorts. "The other guys I've been going out with at least appeared like they wanted to look good. They missed by a mile but they gave it a shot," she told me. "This one didn't give a shit from the get-go."

As Granny told it, she approached with a coy smile, tapped him on the shoulder, and said, "You must be Hank." He then looked at her, slightly bewildered, and explained that he had an appointment he was late for then skedaddled out the door in a flash. I wanted to bitch-slap the old man.

Poor Granny was left at the café without a coffee, date, or clue on WTF this bastard's problem was. She called me from the parking lot to debrief. "If I had to figure it out in the best possible way all around, he was probably overwhelmed for many reasons," she explained, trying to make sense of it. "What a wimp, what a wimp." I was impressed with how well she was holding herself together. If a man pulled that shit with me I would have been crushed, but Granny refused to let her guard down.

"I'm disappointed that he sucks so much, but I think it's on to the next," I said, trying to be optimistic. "Besides, maybe he'll call you and apologize?"

"I don't want to talk to him now," she said definitively. "The game is mine now and I want nothing to do with him. Twice? No man can do this to me twice."

Rejection sucks at any age, but as an older woman the sting is harsher. When you've been out of the game for *decades* and/or accepted your singledom, a slap in the face like that is a huge setback. It makes you question your intentions and goals in the first place. Putting yourself out there in the online world is already a test for your ego, but someone blowing you off online is incomparable to the emotional punch of a face-to-face dismissal.

"Who is *he* to make me feel this way?" she hollered.

We went through possible scenarios to explain Hank's shitty behavior: Maybe her beauty intimidated him (I've seen his picture, she is *way* out of his league). Maybe the realness of the online dating world became too much to handle. Maybe he was really bad at making schedules. Maybe he was afraid of having his heartbroken. Maybe all he really wanted was a phone companion. Whatever the reason, we'll never know. All we could be sure of was that he was a wimp and I hoped he broke out in a bad case of hives.

Hank's behavior was despicable, but there was a silver lining. For the first time I saw in her the glimmer of excitement about meeting someone new. She had been so hesitant, so full of judgment, with her dates, but the truth is, behind her bully facade she was protecting a fragile heart. The moment she let her guard down and opened up to the possibility of finding a true connection she got hurt. He may have been an old sack of farts, but at least Hank got Granny to the place where she could admit to *liking* a man other than Ira and hold out hope for finding something more.

I liked to consider myself a love slave driver, whipping my vibrant granny into romantic shape. Sadly though, the Hank debacle of 2011 brought Granny's dating spirits dangerously low. "I'm feelin' gun-shy, kid," she admitted.

Friends had warned me before we began our online dating journey that there would be tough times and rough patches that would make us want to quit. That's just the nature of putting yourself out there. Sometimes you'll get knocked down. Luckily we both understood that dating isn't a race; there are times when you need a break. As her granddaughter, friend, and wingman, I granted her some space to cool her dating jets.

"There is so much hoopla when we schlep these conversations along, by the time the actual date comes around it's like, eh, I'm tired, I wanna sit on my couch and watch *Desperate Housewives*. The game is different at twenty-five and seventy-five," she said.

Over the following weeks Granny started up a few new conversations with other gentlemen, but none of them panned out. "These men, they're like old tubes of toothpaste, all used up and squeezed out," she said. Although somewhat pessimistic, I was happy to see she was directing her poor dating luck at the men and not on herself. Self-righteous to the core. That's my granny.

# It's Not Me, It's You

**P**ART OF ME FELT like slowing down along with Granny, but the other part of me was getting too much pleasure out of my date-packed weeks. Especially when I was receiving messages from cute boys like Grant, who wrote, "I like your nighttime photo. You look like Giselle in a fashion ad. Which is kind of awesome." Giselle? Yes, that is kind of awesome. Tell me more, Grant.

In his profile he made up a series of questions to answer:

*Favorite Grade in School: 5th.*

*Least Favorite: 9th.*

*If I Had Just One Song to Get the Party Going, Would That Song Be the Macarena?: No.*

I also enjoyed fifth grade and I especially enjoyed that he took it upon himself to do a personal Q&A.

I arrived at 2A, the Alphabet City dive bar, for our date five minutes later than we had planned, but Grant was nowhere in sight. I'm usually very punctual, but I had made a habit of showing up fashionably late for my OkCupid dates.

I'll admit it, it's totally a power play. If I'm late I can avoid sitting at the bar, awkwardly balancing on a stool, trying to maintain good posture and a nonchalant/sexy/intelligent/approachable pout while scanning the crowd on repeat looking for a face that resembles the one I've seen online. I figure that if I give myself a five- to ten-minute window, my date can suffer through those moments rather than me.

Usually my plan works swimmingly. However, this time I was the sucker and Grant was the tardy party. I grabbed a martini and took a seat at a table in the back of the venue. I had to make a friend's going-away dinner after the date, so I was dressed snazzier than I typically would for a Monday-night drink in a dive bar. I had on a sexy purple dress and a pair of dangerously high heels. Sitting alone in a dark corner sipping a cocktail, eyeing around the place all dolled up, I wouldn't have been surprised if someone mistook me for a working girl on the prowl.

Grant entered frazzled, wearing a laid-back flannel. Even though he had chosen the spot, he said he went to a bar ten blocks away "by accident."

He grabbed a drink and sat down. I caught him suspiciously eyeing my outfit. "I'm going to a fancy dinner after this," I stated defensively. "Not that I wouldn't dress like this for you. I mean, I don't know you, but I don't usually wear heels on a Monday, but you know what I mean, right?" Smooth operator, I was not.

I changed the subject. "Where do you live in Bushwick?"

"Off the L." He shrugged. "It's kind of a loft situation."

"What kind of situation is that?"

"One where I have six roommates and one bathroom."

It sounded like a cross between a terrific sitcom and a terrifying nightmare. I only had my one roommate, good ole Huang, and it was almost too much.

Grant had just moved to the city after finishing grad school and wasn't ready to commit to a job, so he'd been spending his time traveling. Lucky dude. He entertained me with an excellent story about a cross-country trip he and a buddy went on over the summer. I tried to relate by sharing a story about a cross-country trip I took with some friends. It was a nightmare; half of us abandoned ship (the Jetta) in Texas, and a friendship was ruined—our experiences were vastly different.

Again we changed the subject. We tried talking about our families and trips we'd been on with them. He told me about a laid-back trip to India with his family last year. I shared details of a chaotic safari in East Africa with my family. I recounted a story about a fight I got into with my sister while in the Serengeti that involved a Maasai warrior, a bow and arrow, and some Xanax. He was clearly freaked out.

Grant is the oldest of five brothers. I am the middle of three sisters. When he found out where I fell in the pecking order, he gave me a look like, "Aha, that explains it."

I'm not sure if it was the dress that was affecting my attitude, but judging by the looks Grant gave me, I'm pretty confident I was exuding some crazy girl vibes.

"What's your last name?" he asked.

"Why? Do you want to google me?"

"No, I'm just curious," he said. Mmmhmm, yeah right. Everyone is a Google stalker, let's be real.

I had to get to my friend's dinner so we said good-bye and parted ways. It was then that I realized we skipped something. He never asked for my number. I didn't expect or necessarily want to go out with him again, but *still* . . . we know my ego needs some stroking. Would it be so much for him to at least feign interest? The lonely hooker was feeling pretty lame.

As I wobbled in my heels to the East Village restaurant to meet my friends, I went over the date in my head and realized Grant did the right thing. Why take a number if you're not going to call? If you're not feeling it, it's more respectable to end things before they begin. I'd rather get dumped before we started something anyway. Saves me time, energy, and breath for bitching. We weren't glaringly compatible. We had, at best, a pleasant drink and conversation, and that's all it would ever be. I appreciated his honest ending to our date.

Of course, I googled him. Unfortunately there was no incriminating dirt. It turns out he's quite the scholar and had a silly haircut in 2008. So what? I didn't need him. I honestly didn't even *like* him—I just liked rejection a whole lot less.

I'm great at justifying things. Eating boxes of cookies, buying that overpriced top, stealing a bottle of vodka—whatever it is, I can find a reason to defend it. After I got Granny's opinion on Grant, I realized where I inherited this trait. Granny managed to turn the situation around so that I was on top, just like we did with Hank. I am her granddaughter; she would make up any bullshit possible to avoid hurt feelings on my end. Rather than admitting the simple fact that he may have just not liked me, Granny dug deep to find every reason in the book to justify his actions. "He hasn't had a job since school?" she asked, clearly ready to bury the unemployed bastard.

"Nope."

"Usually they recruit straight out of grad school for someone in his profession. He must be very troubled," she decided. "He's *stressed* because of his lack of work."

"So it's not me?" I asked, looking for affirmation but also for a laugh.

"Definitely not, he's an insecure man," she said with such certainty it didn't bother me that she had never even met him. "You may have come across too carefree, which he can't take because while you're blowing in the wind, he's got his feet six feet in the ground because he's so stressed out."

I stifled a laugh—she wasn't trying to be funny.

She pushed on. "He spent all this money on extra education and now he's panicked. Poor guy is stressed out." She made a whole narrative about him. It was so convincing I felt like she spent more time with him than I did.

"Yeah, maybe—" I began before Granny cut me off.

"*Maybe* he has another girlfriend and he just came out to play and then he felt guilty and walked away," she hypothesized like a gray-haired Nancy Drew. "There are many ways to analyze this."

I agreed.

"Are you gorgeous? We know yes. Are you smart? We know yes. Are you smart in economics? Maybe not."

"Hey!" I protested.

"You are smart, you are beautiful, you are street smart, you are . . ." She rattled down a list of compliments.

"Don't stop," I said with a giggle. The speed bumps will come, but that's just when your cheerleader/wingman/friend/granny needs to kick into high gear.

# Hakuna Matata

Y ES, I AM RIPPING OFF SIMBA, but the Swahili saying *hakuna matata* really does translate to "no wor-
ries," which is how I feel about my issues when I
travel to Nairobi. All the stresses of everyday life fall to the
wayside, and suddenly I'm not concerned about finding a
man, the asshole who didn't tip at the club, how I'm going to
pay off my Citibank student loans, or that extra five pounds
I'd love to lose. All my attention is on the kids.

Granny's decision to cool her dating jets coincided nicely
with my December trip. It was convenient timing for both
of us to take a break. Every six months I take a hiatus from
city life to visit the kids who I work with in the children's
homes around Nairobi. My time there is divided between
buying textbooks, awarding university scholarships, starting
girls' reading clubs, getting cornrows in my hair, and showing
off the fact that my Jewish nose is long enough for my tongue
to touch it. This may seem like an unusual passion project
for someone who works in a highly sexualized environment
selling overpriced booze. Trust me, the weirdness isn't lost on
me.

My work there started around Christmas 2009, when I met up with Granny, my mother, and two sisters in Kenya to go on a safari. Although Granny had just turned seventy-four, she was in good health with more sass and wit than Khloe Kardashian. This trip, she said, was her dying wish.

Granny and I aren't the only women in our family with caustic personalities and stubborn opinions. Rounding us up in our South Florida home for holidays and graduations can be tumultuous. We're tough critics, picking on one another for choices that range from men to the print on a bikini top. Rendezvousing in Africa for the holidays to sit in tight quarters for extended lengths of time among the animal kingdom seemed like a dangerous choice for us brassy gals. Our poor Tanzanian tour guy, Ramen, was stuck in an estrogen-filled vehicle with us for six long days, after which I'm sure he concluded it would be safer to play with the lions.

Knowing how my family operates, I anticipated the drama. When booking that trip I knew when my neurotic brood left East Africa to spend a final week in Cape Town, I would need an escape plan. I arranged to volunteer at an orphanage in Kayole, a slum in southeast Nairobi where I met and fell in love with a bunch of beautiful and ambitious children.

On that first trip to Kenya in 2009, Charlie and I were still a couple. He'd send me emails every day full of love and support. When we were good, we were good.

Without Charlie's encouragement, I doubt I would have had the drive or ambition to start a nonprofit organization when I returned to the States. I was never the type that aspired to do charity work, but being there and meeting the children changed something in me. The organization was born out of my love for the kids and their obvious need for education, and, in all honesty, a sense of retribution to justify my job in nightlife.

During our breakup, in my downward spiral, I began to reject all responsible adult decisions. I gave up my job in the commercial production company and poured myself into my charity like a wealthy housewife with too much time on her hands. Everything else in my life felt tainted and ugly. The charity was the one thing that made me feel constructive and my time worthwhile.

A year later, in the winter of 2010, I took my second trip to Kenya. Charlie and I had been broken up for six months. While I was in Africa, our romantic emails started up again. We were in the stringing-each-other-along phase. On my way back to the States I *conveniently* had a layover in London. Charlie invited me to stay with him on my way home. I hadn't let go of him yet and certainly wasn't strong enough to turn down an opportunity at seducing him back.

He came to pick me up at the airport. I spotted him waiting in the terminal. It was a scene that had played out dozens of times before in our relationship, during happier times when we were still a pair. The excitement we'd get from running into each other's arms in that same meeting point was like the tear-jerking montage in *Love Actually*, except with more groping and tongue. When I saw him I thought my stomach was going to jump out of my throat from nerves . . . or at least I thought it was nerves.

He grabbed my bags and put his arms around me. I looked up at him, oozing with emotion and sickness, then promptly vomited all over his feet. We stood there in shock, disgusted by my physical reaction to our reunion. "Kenya," I squeaked. "I must have eaten something."

He took me back to his flat. Charlie was no longer living in the cute basement love shack we had cohabited in during my previous trips, the one where we had planned to make a home together. He now shared a high-tech bachelor pad with two other dudes in town. A bachelor pad that I barfed all over—the lawn, kitchen, and bathroom floor. His sickly ex-girlfriend was not the best houseguest in the home of single men. It was as if my body was purging him or Africa or both.

I had to extend my trip for a week because I was too ill to get on a plane. Despite my sickness, we managed to fit in some heavy petting and chats. "I don't want to be with anyone but *you*," he whispered in my ear in between my rushed sprints to the toilet. "The timing isn't good for us now. We need to work on ourselves, but we are going to be together. We have to."

Yes, we *had* to. Maybe it was my fever that was making me delusional enough to buy into his bullshit, but as I lay in his bed, sick as shit, I believed him. When I got back to New York, down on body weight but full on love, I felt happy, revitalized, and skinny. I told myself that we were close to reuniting for good.

Five months later, in the spring of 2011 when I headed back for my Kenya trip in May, I emailed to let him know I'd be *popping* by London on my way back to New York. I had friends in England who I planned to see, but truthfully I expected us to strike back up where we left off. Surely an almost yearlong break was enough. Now it was time to reclaim my man. I was in a delightful state of denial.

"Would love to catch up for coffee but don't think we should stay together," he replied.

*COFFEE?!* I would have preferred he suggest that we drink rat poison while taking turns waxing his back hair and my crotch. We all know what *coffee* means. After getting his email I spent the rest of my time in Kenya obsessively trying to distract myself from him. My work there is emotionally, mentally, and physically demanding. It wasn't hard to fill my head with more constructive thoughts during the day, but at night, lying on my cot trying to sleep, I swatted at mosquitoes and analyzed far too deeply what his message could have meant.

That turned out to be the London trip where over *coffee* he told me he was moving on, beginning to see other people, and I bitch-slapped him. Oy.

*Now* it was December 2011. It had been more than six months since Charlie and I had made any contact and I was deep into my online dating journey when it was time for my next trip to Kenya. "Will you see Charlie?" Granny asked. I could hear the caution in her voice. She didn't want me to undo the months of work that had built up my resistance to him.

"I think so," I confessed. During the seasons since our last contact, I had gone out with dozens of guys, each one slowly breaking down the string I felt bound me to him.

"Don't forget how far you've come, kid," she reminded me. "I'd hate to see you take a step backward." If anyone knows how toxic an encounter with an ex is, it's her.

Enough time had passed that I knew I wasn't in love with Charlie anymore and my dreams where I strangled his Facebook girlfriend in a pool of pudding had almost stopped. "I'll see how I feel after Kenya," I decided.

Whenever I'm in Nairobi I am disconnected from modern-day communication. The electricity is rationed so some days it's not an option to go to the Internet café to check my email or stalk ex, current, or future lovers on the web. When it is working, I'm either too busy or the connection is too slow to even consider logging on to OkCupid or snooping around Facebook.

I rarely use my American phone over there. I learned my lesson after my first trip when my texts and quick calls with Charlie left me with a bill that was higher than my Lower East Side rent. Every night before bed I do a cautionary cell check to make sure there aren't any panicked calls or time-sensitive text messages from Granny or any other concerned parties.

Two weeks into my trip I powered it on before climbing behind my mosquito net when a message appeared from Nate: "Hey, are you back from Kenya yet?"

It had been weeks since I had heard from him and almost a month since our first date. I thought he grew chicken feet and was history. I was prepared to write him off, figuring his "visa" excuse had worked on me. I was impressed that he even remembered I was going to Kenya and furthermore that he was getting in touch while I was there.

"Nope, I'll be back next Monday," I replied, feeling cagey and confused.

"Hope the trip goes well. I want to see you when you're back," he texted immediately. I stared at my iPhone, a device that looks beyond foreign in my home in Kenya. That studly Australian man is messaging me while I'm in Kenya?

That night, rather than lying up with Charlie on my mind, I thought about Mr. Australian, Mr. Cerebral, Mr. Asshole, Mr. Rebound, Mr. Player, Mr. Friend, Mr. Traveler, Mr. Artist, Mr. Scenester, and all the other guys I had been out with post-Charlie and the progress I had made. I was impressed with myself that I had barely thought about Nate since our date. It wasn't because I wasn't into him—I definitely was, probably more than I wanted to admit to myself—but I was learning to manage my expectations and refusing to let my thought-space be clouded by thoughts of men and the future. I was living in the present and comfortable in my own company.

When I got to London for my layover, I stayed with my friend Julia. We went out like two wild teenagers on spring break. Dancing with strange men in the pub below her flat, one leaned in and kissed me and I didn't stop him. It was the first time I ever felt free in Charlie's city.

The next day I decided to email Charlie and ask him to meet for lunch. We spent four years of our lives together as friends, lovers, and partners. I didn't want to throw that out and I especially didn't want to make the mistake Granny had with Ira. I was beginning to see that the problem wasn't that they should have been together for all those years instead of on their own or married to their spouses. What they should have done was found more closure back in the '80s rather than wasting decades on regret. I may have handled my breakup like a pouty brat, but I was ready to unleash some white doves and make peace.

We caught up on our lives over eggs. I was relieved that he didn't bring up my violent physical outburst from our previous meeting. Although I had moved on from him romantically, his company was something I still very much craved. The grieving process felt as though it was almost over. He was no longer the love of my life; rather he was just a man who tried to love me and I tried to love back. Part of me missed him, but it was the idea of him and the memories we had.

We had shared so much love and so many adventures, but we outgrew each other. I was genuinely glad to hear that he was doing well and was happy in his relationship. He was with someone who shared his goals and plans for the future. I didn't want to dwell on him anymore. I had too many exciting things ahead of me.

The night I landed back in New York, I had butterflies in my stomach. As most New Yorkers can attest, the skyline has that effect. As I stared off at the memory-filled metropolis, my phone buzzed. It was Nate. "Hey sweetheart, welcome home. Can I take you out this week?"

Damn. He was good. Too good? As a cynical young lady I was confused by Nate's effort. I had been pushing Granny to be more open, but it was beginning to occur to me that I was just as guilty of fearing intimacy and the possibility of finding something real.

# He's Busy? You're Twice as Busy

**G**RANNY HAD SPENT ENOUGH time playing hooky from her dating life and mulling over the Hank-Bermuda-shorts encounter while I was away. It was time to step up my wingman game and get back to bullying.

"You're not getting any younger," I teased.

"You and me both," she giggled.

"What do you have cooking on Match and JDate?"

"I find that all these old people—forget me—the *other* old people, they just like to *talk*." Granny was growing frustrated after engaging in a game of phone tag with Jay, her newest prospect from JDate.

"So talk to him," I encouraged. "Is a phone call really that painful? You love talking on the phone. You call me at least twice a day."

"I call you because you're my flesh and blood," she hollered. "I'm not interested in a telephone affair, and that's what all these schmucks are after."

I piped up in his defense. "It's important to talk to someone for ten to fifteen minutes before a date." It doesn't necessarily have to be a phone call, but some sort of extended communication, whether it's an email exchange or text banter, is helpful in discerning if someone is a real prospect prior to making a date commitment.

"Ten to fifteen minutes?" she asked sarcastically. "You're living in a dreamland. They're still stuttering their names after ten minutes. These are old people. Ten to fifteen minutes in the world of twenty-five-year-olds is an hour of conversation. Ten to fifteen minutes with an old fart of eighty or older goes on forever. I told him he could call me in the evenings after nine," she said as if she was making a compromise with me.

"Calling after nine is not just late for older people, that's dangerously close to booty-call territory."

This argument only wound Granny up tighter. "Listen, I do things, I don't sit around all night," she hollered. "I move my body and go. He wants to talk to me? I don't have time to chat. I'm *charming*; he has to come and meet me." In case anyone was wondering where my confidence comes from, wonder no further.

Luckily Jay did want to talk to her and, even further, get to know her in person. After a successful "ten- to fifteen-minute" call they made plans to meet for a meal. Driving to the date, Granny's car got stuck between two bridges along the intercoastal. She took this time to call me and complain about the restaurant he chose. "I hate TooJay's."

This was a blatant lie. It is actually me who hates TooJay's. Whenever I visit Granny in Florida, she insists on at least one trip to the gourmet deli known for its senior clientele and pastrami. I reminded her of this. "Only for breakfast, I only like their breakfast. It's already past twelve, this is clearly a lunch date," she insisted.

"Go wild, order breakfast for lunch."

"Only old people eat at TooJay's," she whined.

"You are old," I reminded her. "Hip but old." This was part of Granny's predate routine. She's like the skinny girl complaining that she's fat. Even though she knows she's a size zero, she still needs me to remind her that she has no cellulite. She hung up. I could tell she was nervous, perhaps fearing another blow-off situation.

I kept my phone close to my side in case disaster struck again, but I didn't hear from her until two hours had passed and her date was through. Her debriefing began: "If you spent twenty-four hours with the guy, twenty-three would be about him." I was glad to hear they already had something in common.

They started off the date by fessing up about their real ages. Apparently both of them had taken some liberties and fibbed on their profiles. Jay was eighty-one and impressed by Granny's looks. "You look damn good," he told her.

"I know," she replied without a shred of modesty.

She confided to me, "I told him he did too, but it was a lie."

"He's five years older than you," I reminded her.

"Going on six," she snapped. "Make a long story short, he looks like a prune face." She paused for a reaction, but I refused to give one. "What do I mean by prune face? It's shaped like a prune and it's lined like a prune. With deep wrinkles all through his face."

"You are old, that's what happens! People get wrinkled!"

"Yes, of course, but he's got more than anyone I've ever been with. I've been with *older* men but none with so many *lines.*" She could sense my eyes rolling over the phone. For my sake, she tried changing her tune. "He is healthy, however, and he's got no special meds to speak of, which is rare for people of our age."

Once she had comfortably released some solid complaints from her system, she began to divulge more about the positives of Jay. They were from the same area in New York; both had only one child, had traveled to many of the same places, and shared several interests. Despite her toughest intentions, she sounded pretty smitten.

Then she cleared her throat, pausing for emphasis. "Are you ready for the real kicker?"

"Hit me."

"I lost my tooth, my front tooth, mid-date."

Aha, and suddenly it became clear why she was trying to bury him: the lady was embarrassed. Granny has a movie-star smile, which is the product of movie-star maintenance. She had veneers put in years ago, which, although looking killer, at times fall out.

"What?" I asked, part horrified, part amused.

"Yup. You told me to go with breakfast. So I got one of those bagels. You know, with the lox and the cream cheese? I take one bite, and what do you know? My top front tooth falls right out."

I tried to stifle my giggles. "Oh God, what did you do?"

"I said to myself, 'You lost your tooth. Don't be obvious and don't swallow it.' The tooth had other plans. It popped straight out of my lips and onto the plate." We both broke out into hysterical laughter. Granny and I share the ability to laugh at ourselves even in the most humiliating situations. This quality is perhaps one of the best that Granny has imparted to me.

Luckily Jay was a like-minded individual. He looked at

her and said, "Please don't be embarrassed. I don't mind a bit. I'm enjoying every moment of being with you." My heart melted.

He thoughtfully picked up their conversation from where they left off like a true gentleman. From the sounds of it, they really got along. "I actually enjoyed his company," she said, surprising both of us.

"He asked me to call him, but I said, 'I don't think so, mister, you call me, that's how it works.'" Albeit old-fashioned, I agreed. I'm all about being a modern woman, but I think nine times out of ten, men should make the first move. It's old school and über traditional, but if it ain't broke, why fix it? If a man wants to see you he's going to make an effort to see you. If he doesn't, he won't.

"When we said good-bye, I extended my arm to shake his hand but he hugged me. A big hug, a prune sandwich!"

It was a promising date, but we knew better than to get our hopes up too quickly. Granny wasn't able to admit to herself yet that she was crushing on him. Playing it extra cautious after Hank's dismissal of her, she was curbing her interest by clinging to superficial arguments like the lines on his face or his chatty nature. We were getting *too* good at suspending excitement when it came to a good prospect.

Later that week, on a cold mid-December evening, I took Nate up on his offer for a second date. He met me outside my apartment to stroll up to Upstate, an oyster bar in the East Village. As I walked out of my building, I caught him nervously checking out his reflection in a car window. "You trying to steal that car?" I called out to him.

He smiled and came in to lay a wet one on me. He was

better looking and somehow taller than I remembered—I
know those are definitely positive qualities, but my attraction
to him made me uneasy.

Grabbing my hand, he led me to the restaurant and
we caught up on the past month of our lives. He had been
swamped with work. His bar was set to open the month prior
but building inspections and construction were taking longer
than he'd expected. In my head I saw myself getting involved
with someone who was far outside the reaches of nightlife,
but here was this man who was about to build his career on
it. It was hypocritical to the core, I know, but I still had my
guard up after his bout of forgetfulness that we started out on.
If things were going to move forward, I needed to let go of the
"lecherous bar owner" stereotype I had in my head.

Sitting at the wooden bar, we smashed dozens of oysters
and pints of beer. I told him about the kids in Kenya. He
asked such insightful questions it was hard not to be wooed.
He had a genuine and attentive way of listening that made
me feel like I was the most important gal in the world. His
hazel eyes would lock with mine with such sincerity it made
me blush. It was a great date, no denying it, but *again* I didn't
hear from him the next day or the day after.

I gave Granny the dish, going back and forth with myself
over whether I cared if he ever called again. "Take a breath,
kid," she advised. "If you do, you do. If you don't, you don't.
It really is that simple." Ah, the old and the wise, they make it
sound so easy.

Using the tool of distraction, Granny told me about Roger,
an eighty-two-year-old JDater. She responded to a message he
sent and now was waiting for a reply to plan a date. Originally
he wrote:

"I happen to be a very nice man!!!! I am seeking a very nice lady to share good times with. Just a little about me is that I am a caring, considerate, kind & gentle, romantic and very sensual person!!! So if you would like to meet and say hello, let me know."

Based off his unbridled use of exclamation points and his self-proclaimed characteristics of considerate (and sensual . . .), you would think she would have heard back from him immediately, right? Nope.

"I've been reading the magazines, you know, the articles," she said. "They say men these days call soonest one to two weeks. *At least* ten days. Women call the next day. Men, they think about it for a while, maybe they get rid of another woman they've been seeing. They're calling it 'the New Way of Dating.'"

I was not a fan of this new wave romance. "I'm not down with playing games." I had already waited over a month from our first date; another two weeks wasn't going to cut it.

"It's the same games at every age. Get used to it."

"But I hate sitting around waiting for a call. It feels pathetic," I admitted.

"Who said to wait around? I certainly didn't." She giggled. "He's busy? Honey, you're *twice* as busy."

Perhaps the most valuable tip in the dating game. Nothing good comes from waiting around. How are you going to win the lottery if you don't get off your ass and buy a ticket? I decided to make myself busy with Drew, an OkCupider who responded to the line in my profile: "*You Should Message Me If: You're not creepy and you are wearing a shirt in your pic.*"

> **Him:** All I have to do is be shirtful for you to love me huh? That's easy. Hi there, I'm Drew. Hi. Hi. Hi.

**Me:** Hi. Hi. Hi. I never promised love in exchange for a
shirt, but it helps.


And so it began. We bantered back and forth for few a
days before locking down a date. I suggested meeting at Von,
a chill downtown wine bar, but he told me we couldn't go
there because it would be "awkward" for him because of an
"incident" with one of their bartenders. Despite the red flags
he was sending my way, I would not relent.

We ended up meeting at a heavily holiday-decorated
Union Square bar of his choice, one where he had safely not
slept with any of the staff. When I arrived he was waiting
at the bar with a bottle of wine like a pro. Bold move—not
only did he pick our poison but he got a whole bottle, which
meant multiple drinks.

Our get-to-know-you bit quickly escalated into entertaining reenactments of other OkCupid dates and reveals on past
relationships. Typically I wouldn't recommend that kind of
chat for a first date, but it was comical, and since I already
knew he had a promiscuous streak, it felt organic.

"I date older women; you're too young for me," he said
with a sideways smile. He was thirty-four and I was twenty-
four—facts we already knew from our profiles. He was trying
reverse psychology on me. I grew up with Granny; I am no
stranger to this technique.

We spent the majority of the date criticizing each other.
He didn't like my shirt. I didn't like his tie. I didn't believe he
was really six-one. He didn't like the neighborhood I live in.
"I can see why you need to be online dating," he teased.

"I can guess why you need to overcompensate with arrogance."

The bickering went back and forth, falling somewhere between silly and sadistic. By the end of the date I wasn't sure if we were buds, enemies, or potential lovers, but I had a feeling if we were on a playground, he'd be chasing me and pulling my pigtails.

I expected to hear more from Drew in the days following our date but I didn't. I wasn't even sure if I liked him after our drinks, but when I didn't hear back from him I began to wonder.

"Do you think I should text Drew and/or Nate?" I asked Granny, hoping she would give the green light.

"No way."

"But I am a modern woman. I make modern moves," I argued, although I already knew she was right.

"Scarcity makes everything more in demand," she said.

This is a theory Granny has imparted on me many times using a real estate analogy: If there's a building full of empty apartments, the buying price is low. If there are only a few apartments left and people are buying fast, the price shoots up. Simple economics. The same rules apply in the laws of attraction.

"Follow me, I will flee; flee from me, I will follow" is a French saying that a male friend shared with me years ago. As soon as you pull back, they want you more.

"Remember Jay the Prune Face?" Granny asked. "If he likes me he's really playing his cards right."

"I thought you weren't that into him?"

"Well, I wasn't, but now that I haven't heard from him I'm liking him more and more," she said. "If he called me now I'd probably have to stop myself from panting into the receiver and proposing marriage."

· · ·

The game Granny had me playing worked. It was like waiting for time to pass. If you stare at the clock it can feel like ages, but if you keep busy it flies by. By distracting myself, keeping active with dates and friends, my eyes weren't on the clock.

The following week when Nate finally texted to meet up, I was at a Christmas party at subMercer, a brick-walled cellar in SoHo. I declined his offer. I wasn't going to go out of my way to make myself available to him. I was genuinely *busy*.

"Sorry, I'm already out tonight," I texted.

"How about tomorrow?" he replied

"I'll be working but you're welcome to come by." I was trying to *appear* indifferent.

The next night, as I stood by the bar chatting with a friend, I saw Nate come in. He was significantly more sober than the first time I saw him at the club. "Do you think you'll remember seeing me here tonight?" I teased. He smiled and pulled me in to plant a kiss on my cheek.

*What are you doing?* I thought. *You really want to fall for a guy again? And then what? You get hurt.*

I got him and his buddies a bucketful of beers, then ignored them for the rest of the night. Before leaving he kissed me good-bye and I tried to tell myself to forget him.

# Dasher and Dancer

THE NEXT NIGHT WAS Christmas Eve and I was stuck in the club serving booze to the wealthy Jews and Christians who had nowhere better to be. Since it was a holiday, we had to dress up. Any excuse to go all out with a theme is big in nightlife. For Halloween the previous year, I dressed as a "sexy baby," clothed in an adult-sized diaper and pasties; I put all the sexy cops, sexy cats, and sexy witches to shame. For this particular holiday, my fellow servers were all clothed in different versions of the "sexy Santa" costume, while I opted for a fur vest, fur gloves, and red paint on my nose. I was one silly-looking reindeer.

Nate messaged, asking if I had seen a gray scarf that he had left behind at the club the night before. Looking back, this could have been a tactful bullshit excuse to strike up conversation.

Scanning the dimly lit club's lost and found, I spotted a scarf that could have been gray. I told him I had it, but upon further inspection in the light I noticed that it was actually purple and rather ladylike. "I found *a* scarf but I don't think it's *your* scarf," I texted.

"I do need a new scarf . . ." he replied.

"I wouldn't want your neck to be cold . . ."

"Would you mind if I came by to get it?"

"No, but I should warn you I'm dressed very furry and very weird tonight."

"I LOVE furry and weird."

Nate busted in the joint, walked right up to me, and kissed me on the mouth in front of his friends and mine. My face turned redder than the tray of vodka cranberries I was holding. I weakly handed him the scarf.

"It's not mine, but I'll take it," he whispered in my ear.

"Consider it an early Christmas gift."

Since it was a holiday, the club was slow, and instead of looking after tables I got to hang with Nate. I had to stop worrying about what would happen next and start enjoying the moment.

That night my stomach hurt from laughing so hard as he swung me around the dance floor and made me pretend to audition for the Pussycat Dolls. I was letting go and beginning to fall for him. I already knew he had plenty of positive qualities, but I hadn't seen this fun side of him. I began to grasp how important that was for me in a partner. I'm a weird girl, there's no denying it, and I wanted a guy with a free spirit and a killer sense of humor. I didn't realize that I had a checklist in my head for what I was looking for in a guy until I noticed Nate ticking them off.

He took one of my furry gloves for himself and declared the night the best Teen Wolf Jew-mas in history. At the end of my shift he threw me over his shoulder like an ogre (cross that off the bucket list), and in the cold Christmas night he carried me back across the Lower East Side to his apartment where we had some drunk but *fun* sex.

"You are so beautiful," he told me.

I was hooked.

# The Horizontal Boogie

Sex changes everything, or so we've been told.
The morning after doing the horizontal Christmas
boogie, I tried to resist following my hormonal im-
pulses. My first time knockin' boots with Nate wasn't going to
change *everything*, but it certainly did change some things.

When Charlie and I broke up, I could count my number
of sexual partners on one hand. I'd always been a relationship
kind of girl. Or, at the very least, a know-your-last-name-and-
share-a-few-meals-before-getting-naked kind of girl. Coupled
with my paralyzing fear of herpes and other unsightly STDs,
I did a good job of keeping my legs crossed throughout my
early adult life.

Although my encounter with José, the sentimental
scenester, was disappointing on many levels, there was one
positive outcome: I learned I could have "no strings attached"
sex. That may make me sound like a hussy (I'm not), but it
was liberating and helped me get over Charlie and learn how
to enjoy my sexuality after our break up.

If I slept with someone and it was good, I enjoyed the experience but reminded myself that there's a lot more involved

for me to actually *like* him (regardless of the nagging messages my vagina is sending to my brain). And if the sex was bad, I had become freakishly good at erasing it from my memory immediately after it occured. A dick the size of a jalapeño pepper that humped me like a jackhammer? I have no idea what or who you are referring to.

"I wish it was as acceptable when I was your age as it is now," Granny said about doing the deed. "I'm not promoting promiscuity. But if the sex is bad, *why go further?*" By experiencing this trial-and-error process with men post-Charlie, I learned how right she was.

It had been a year and a half from the time that Charlie and I initially broke up to me boinking Nate. During that time I had sexual partners (let's not use numbers . . . ), but that's all they ever were. My hookups were great for scratching the itch, but I was never (probably intentionally) sleeping with anyone who I could imagine being in a real relationship with.

Granny and I have always been able to talk about *everything*. However, when it comes to sex we save the nitty-gritty details and stick to the basic "Did you do it or not?" line of questioning. Let's face it, no matter how close you are, it'd be weird to talk size, shape, and technique with your grandma.

"I'm worried about your sister," Granny once told me after my older sister and her boyfriend hit the two-year mark in their relationship. "I think she might actually marry Greg."

"Why? What's wrong with Greg?" We all love her boyfriend. They're a stellar pair.

"I *love* Greg, but if she marries him I'm concerned she won't have had enough opportunities with other men"—she paused for emphasis—"*sexually.*"

"She's had other boyfriends . . . and I'm sure *experiences* before."

"Not enough," Granny concluded. I love that she doesn't cling to the traditional view where one should wait for marriage or limit oneself to a mere few lovers over a lifetime.

Although I may have done a solid job of painting myself as a lush, loose lady, I truthfully hadn't had sex with any of the guys I had met on the dating sites because: a) I wasn't online dating to get laid—I was doing it to move past the quick fix of sex and looking for something more genuine and substantial; b) I hadn't met anyone who I was *both* physically and mentally attracted to; and c) many of the attractive online daters gave off heavy player vibes and there is nothing I hate more than letting a player get his way.

Adam was one such sleazeball. He was one of the first guys I had gone out with from OkCupid and exemplified wholeheartedly what many of the online suitors were after. His game was so obvious; even if I weren't a weary woman of nightlife I would have picked up on his moves.

"You're really beautiful," he uttered seductively as I went to take my first sip of Rioja. I was caught off guard—instead of putting the glass to my mouth I tilted it, and the wine spilled all over my lap.

I was stained, wet, and slightly embarrassed, yet this was only a marginally awkward moment of our date.

About five minutes into our get-to-know-you chat Adam asked me to state my strengths and weaknesses. That's pretty serious territory to tread when one hasn't even finished her first half-spilled glass of wine. I thought I'd lighten it up by translating strengths to party tricks.

I recited pi. I have the first fifty digits committed to memory. I know not everyone would consider that a strength—

few would even call it a party trick—but it was the best I could come up with. He didn't look impressed. "Anything else?" he asked.

I can also make a raspberry sound for a crazy long amount of time. I demonstrated. Again, I'm not sure if that qualifies as a talent but I wasn't performing in a Miss Universe pageant and I had just met this guy and didn't feel like rattling off a list of my best qualities.

He crinkled his nose. "Do you have Asperger's?" he asked. I shook my head. Adam leaned in and smirked—he was eager to overshare: "I'm really good at sex."

"Really?" I leaned in, feigning enthusiasm. "Would you say it's the technique you have down or size?"

He blushed. "Both, I guess."

"Okay, show me with your hands." I gestured. "Is it this big or this big or *this* big?" I dramatically moved my hands closer and farther apart.

He blushed harder and looked away. "Forget it, I don't need to tell you that."

I totally agreed. He didn't need to tell me any of that. It was inappropriate, and although I'm sure it was meant to turn me on, it absolutely did not.

When I told Granny about Adam's "strength," her protective instincts kicked in. "Sounds like a creep," she snarled.

"I left after thirty minutes."

"You stayed twenty-five minutes too long," she said. "You gotta treat these encounters like one of those speed-dating whatchamacallits. You give him five minutes to prove himself. If he's a schlub or a freak you say, 'Bye-bye, nice knowin' ya,' then flee."

Boy, was I glad I had chosen to give Nate more than five

minutes of my time. It didn't hurt that he was the tallest guy I had ever been with. I could finally fulfill my lifelong fantasy of climbing up a man like a jungle gym. Considering it was our first rendezvous in the nude, I was more than pleasantly surprised. However, I knew I still needed to keep my hormones in check.

The morning after our sexual encounter was Christmas Day. He woke up in a panic, late for a holiday brunch with his Australian friends. Clearly the Jewish American in his bed, dressed as slutty reindeer/Teen Wolf with smudges of red paint (lipstick) still on her nose, was not invited. As he planted a rushed kiss on my mouth before ducking in a cab, I braced myself with the fact that I might not hear from him until after the New Year.

My family was in the city for the holiday. Granny and my mom love hooking into the Jewish cliché of noshing on dumplings at a crowded Chinese restaurant in Manhattan while all the goys sit around a Christmas tree sipping eggnog. I met them by their hotel near Times Square for dinner. Granny took one look at me and said, "You've been with a lover."

"What?" I blushed. "No. Who? What? Why would you say—"

She smirked. "You can't play a player, kid."

"Who is he?" my mom asked excitedly. Moms always want to get in on the scoop, but it's easier for me to be more candid with Granny.

"No one, no one," I assured them. He really was still no one, definitely not worthy of a roundtable interrogation topic by my family.

Granny winked and nodded at me, as if to say, "Mmmhmm, I'll get the dish later." My mom narrowed her stare in on me, suspecting something was up. Both my sisters rolled their eyes, totally disinterested.

My family, excluding me, loves musicals. After dim sum we went to see *Priscilla Queen of the Desert* on Broadway. The musical takes place in Australia. The accents of the brightly sequined drag queens did not help to quiet my Nate-driven thoughts.

I had my phone switched off during the performance, but as soon as it was over I powered it on and almost peed myself when I saw he had texted: "My holiday is almost over but I'd like to hook into this Hanukkah thing."

Humana humana humana. I gave a big yawn and told my family I was pooped and needed to head back downtown. Granny gave me another one of her all-knowing winks and whispered, "Enjoy your *lover.*"

I met Nate at Eight Mile Creek, an Australian bar in SoHo, where he and all his friends were watching cricket. Apparently it's an Australian tradition to watch the game on Christmas. Hot men from Down Under with big bats and white suits? Sure, I could totally get into cricket. He handed me a pint of beer and introduced me as "my *friend* Kayli" to all of his pals.

I knew I was not his girlfriend, but it was an uncomfortable introduction that made me squirm with each fresh handshake. I guess we were *friends*, but I preferred Granny's title of *lovers* more. After the game we wandered back through SoHo, passing the darkened storefronts, to his apartment, stopping every block or so to make out.

Back at his place we went for round two of pin the Aussie on Kayli, but again in the morning he had to rush out of the house. He was headed upstate with a group of buddies for a manly wilderness week. Outside his building we said good-bye; he awkwardly gave me two high-fives, an aggressive fist bump, and flashed me the peace sign before turning down the block. *What the hell was that?* I thought.

As soon as I walked into my apartment Granny called. "Who were you sleeping with?" were the first words out of her inquisitive mouth.

"The Australian."

"Do you still like him?"

"Yeah—" I began, unsure of where she was headed.

"Oh good." She breathed a sigh of relief. "If you slept with him and still like him, it must have been good. I hate it when it's the other way around."

Although Granny can talk a good game, as far as she'll confide in me, she is no longer getting her feathers ruffled down below. She's far from a prude when it comes to her sexual views, but the idea of getting naked with an older man, most likely with a hip replacement, isn't something she's interested in. "Bed relationships at this age have got to be an experience and a half. I don't look forward to dealing with an old, messy, farty situation. I've had *very* nice relationships in the bedroom in my life. I'm not about to ruin that with a wobbly sack of bones." TMI, Granny.

Ever since Viagra hit the market, the rate of sexual activity among older folks has spiked. However, just because it's all the rage in the senior communities doesn't mean that Granny is a horny sheep following the flock. I respect her decision to keep her clothes on. She's sneaky, so there is always the chance that she's getting some and keeping it to herself, but I doubt it.

At seventy-six, sex might not even be in the picture. Intimacy is not so much about rubbing, humping, and grinding, although it can be. Instead it's something that evolves out of a human connection, shared experiences, and unending patience. "What I'm realizing is that when you're older, because sex is minimal or a nonexistent part of the equation, you really need to *like* each other. The physical part becomes less and less important. It's the character that matters so much more," she said.

At twenty-four, sex is not only in the picture, it's the frame, backing, and nail in the wall. While my *friend* Nate was away on his country excursion, I didn't see any reason for me to withhold from playing the field. I knew I liked him, but he still wasn't my boyfriend. Maybe it was my fear of commitment or my enjoyment of indulging in online dates, or perhaps that I hadn't made up my mind about him yet, but I still had a dating profile and I intended to use it.

I made plans to grab a drink with Ben at Vbar on St. Mark's. He was handsome and his profile was filled with pictures of him traveling all over the world. Prior to our date I had dinner with girlfriends. I obviously couldn't leave before dessert. Sweet potato donuts? Come on, you would have stayed too.

Because of the donuts, I was fifteen minutes late to meet Ben, which is beyond fashionably late, it's just plain rude. But when I arrived Ben didn't mind. He shot me a warm smile and shook my hand. When he started talking I realized he had an accent, an Israeli accent. Heart be still. I love hummus, tanned skin, and salty seas. Nowhere on his profile did it mention his international roots. *Score!*

Accents in general are always a perk, but Israelis, ah . . . with their dark, brooding features and intense eyes. He reminded me of a guy I dated when I was eighteen and first moved to the city. I suddenly got bashful in his presence.

Ben had a nose like Owen Wilson, all mangled and weird. I loved it. I once dated a guy with a nose and chin that almost touched. My friends nicknamed him "Fortune Cookie Face." Unlike the Adonis-esque perfection of Nate's looks, Ben fell into that category of sexy/ugly, a category that I quite like.

Our conversation flowed more organically than most of my dates. He was the type of guy who works to live, a quality I admire. He had been making a lot of changes in his life over the past seven months. No more cigarettes, green juice diets, Bikram yoga, etc. When I asked what the impetus was for the change, he confessed, "I just got divorced."

A recent divorcé might scare away many a young lady, but not this nut job. Over the summer in LA I went to see a psychic in Santa Monica who told me I was going to be a second wife. Being a second wife sounded pretty first rate to me. I'm not against the idea of settling down one day with a guy who had already failed at marriage, had learned from his mistakes, and was coming back to the table with more knowledge, understanding, compassion, etc. (Okay, it's a dark theory with possibly flawed logic and many obvious holes, but I need to justify the psychic's prediction.)

New to the dating world, after being with the same woman for ten years, Ben said he was enjoying his bachelor lifestyle and, with his Israeli accent, he described himself as a "newborn hedonist." Clearly I was into it. He told me I was the second girl he'd been out with from OkCupid but assured me he had *great* luck with the first.

"What happened?" I of course had to ask.

He went out with Raquel, a journalist who writes about S&M parties. From what I gathered, Raquel was a wild child. On their second date she brought him to a party where he watched her get down with two other ladies in front of a room-

ful of people. *Oh, Raquel!* I was obviously shocked by this information for a few reasons: a) What qualities did Raquel and
I have in common in our profiles that he thought to ask us
both out? b) How come I'd been living in New York for almost seven years and had yet to be invited to an S&M party?

Be careful what you wish for . . . Ben mistook my school-
girl curiosity as a desire to join. "You know, I think Raquel
would like you a lot," he said with a sly smile on his crooked
face. "Would you want to come to a party with us?" I changed
my mind. I definitely didn't want to be invited to the party.
Parties? I hate parties. Parties are the worst.

I decided to call it quits on the date before Raquel showed
up with her leather bustier and metal-studded thong, crack-
ing her whip. I like to think of myself as adventurous when it
comes to sex, but an online dating orgy was not something on
my bucket list.

When I told Granny about Ben and his rendezvous with
Raquel, she was more than open-minded. "He's a man, of
course he went. You can't hold that against him."

I was surprised by her lack of judgment. She was so accepting, almost too accepting.

"Have you been to a sex party?" I asked suspiciously.

She gasped. "Never, never, never." Then, "Oh, I went to
one but I didn't know I was going to a sex party. I was seventeen years old."

The lady is full of surprises.

"I didn't stick around for the fun and games," she swore.
(I'm sure I'd tell my granddaughter the same thing . . .) "I was
dating a man who brought me, and once I realized what was
going on I asked him to take me home. Crazy stuff, kid, crazy
stuff."

"Wow." I was totally impressed and slightly jealous that Granny once again out-cooled me.

Granny was so unprejudiced toward Ben she even suggested I go out with him again. "I don't fault him. He's an Israeli and they do it all. On top of it, he's a guy."

I love that unlike most grandmothers who would encourage their twenty-four-year-old granddaughters to commit to a relationship, or, at the very least, not encourage casual sex, what Granny wants for me is more experiences. Whether they're outrageous or meaningful, they're a part of life.

Ben was a funny distraction that I appreciated since I hadn't heard a peep from Nate during his trip. A week had passed since our fist bump on the street, and it was now New Year's Eve. Although Nate was on my mind, there was no way in hell I was going to be the first one to send a message. In the virtual chase, I wanted to be the hunted not the hunter.

It had been quite a year. The good, the bad, and the ugly. "Embrace it all," Granny wisely advised. "Here's to new men, new experiences, new adventures, new relationships, new laughs, and new loves."

New Year's Eve is a big night to go out in New York. It beats Halloween and Fourth of July with its hype and crowds. For weeks prior, everyone asks what your plans are, who you're going to spend it with, what your resolutions are going to be, and have you bought a hot glittery dress yet? If you're single, you of course are wondering if there will be a special someone for you to swap spit with when the clock reaches midnight. A kiss to start off the year, ooh la la. So romantic, so cliché . . . but, admittedly, so much what I wanted.

To bring in 2012, like many New Year's Eves prior, I shuffled around the club swinging sparklers, popping bottles, avoiding creeps, and trying not to slap crazy-drunk girls in sequined bandage dresses. It might sound lame, but I enjoy working on the holiday because it takes the pressure off the night, you make good money, avoid the hectic lines where you freeze your ass off, and drink for free. Cha-ching.

I also love watching drunk people—it's better than going to the zoo. On New Year's Eve people get wasted. Bopping to the music, getting snippy, walking into walls, shamelessly flirting. It's adorable until they start giving the waitress lip. I decided to take a page out of Granny's notebook. Whenever someone started in with some attitude, I told them with wide, sincere eyes, "Listen, I'm a little bit of a witch." This is something Granny tells me when she wants respect. On New Year's Eve people are superstitious; telling them I'm a witch worked. "I have a feeling 2011 was sort of shitty for you, huh?" They nod. "But it's weird, I have this crazy intuition that 2012 is going to be different. This is *your* year." Suddenly they're on my team—with hope and witchcraft I have won them over.

In all my years in New York I've never been as single as I was New Year's Eve 2011. Of course I had Nate and my string of dates that I had been toying around with, but there was no commitment, no required or expected midnight kiss. There was just me and my open mind, open heart, and occasionally open legs. It may sound lame, but it was actually liberating to have absolutely no real expectations. My lips could kiss anyone they wanted. At midnight they went for my best friends. My single ladies came in to keep me company at work and bring in the New Year. We happily danced, played, drank, and laughed. (Yes, I was working. No, I was not doing a good job.) As the clock struck midnight we kissed, then followed my Colombian friend's tradition of stuffing money in our inside-out yellow panties and eating twelve grapes. (My friend, who legitimately might be a witch because of all her traditions, supplied the necessary props.)

I would have been content with my friends' kisses and company, but sometimes when you keep expectations low you get to be pleasantly surprised. Around 3 a.m. I spotted a large Australian leaning by the bar wearing a little bow tie and a big grin.

"I came for a New Year's kiss," he said, pulling me into him.

"How was your trip?" I asked, trying to appear nonchalant.

"Good, but I missed you." Hot tamales. Something about that accent of his just made me want to slap myself across the face.

He took me home at the end of the night and we had sex. Really. Good. Sex. Sex that made me contemplate if things were really beginning to change. I didn't want to get carried away in my head with what we were and where we stood and if he was my man or my friend or my lover or man/lover/friend/sex toy. I was simply enjoying his company and how he made me feel romantically and, of course, sexually.

It might be cliché and he was still way too good-looking, but goddamn, it was a great way to kick off 2012.

"He came to you on New Year's?" Granny asked suspiciously.

"Sure did," I gloated.

"And you spent the night with him?"

"Sure did," I gloated some more.

"Well, it sounds like you're his main squeeze. A man spends New Year's with the girl he fancies the most."

# Friends in a Hopeless Place

A FTER NEW YEAR'S NATE CONFESSED his undying love and begged me to be his life partner, and we quickly entered into a deeply committed monogamous relationship state of bliss. Psych.

Even if that had been the reality, I'm not confident I would have been prepared or open emotionally, mentally, or romantically to deal with it. The present was so good that I wasn't so concerned with the future. We were starting something, but it was still unclear whether he'd be my winter hookup or the future father of my five children.

As Granny eloquently put it: "Listen, kid, you're not flowers yet. The two of you, you're budding roses."

Through January and February we started to *date* each other. Nate didn't just call me late at night to come over or text me to meet up for a quick drink among friends. He was actually *dating* me and the boy was pretty damn good at it. He took me to the rodeo at Madison Square Garden and we dressed up like cowboys. We went bowling at the Gutter in Williamsburg. There was an Australian Day costume party where we covered each other in body paint to dress up as

Gotye and Kimbra from the "Somebody That I Used to Know" video. Ever have a man paint your body or paint a man's? Let's just say it is a highly intimate process with many crevices and bulges to navigate.

Despite all the fun activities we were getting up to and feelings we were developing, I knew he wasn't my boyfriend. How did I know? He made it pretty obvious. He *still* introduced me to his pals as his "friend Kayli," *always* with the prefix. Then there were days when I didn't hear from him at all. Whenever I felt him pulling back, I pulled back more. Albeit game-y, I stuck firmly to Granny's "He's busy? You're twice as busy" maxim.

I wasn't so invested that if things fell apart I'd spend months bitching to Granny or hunting for another vulnerable club rat to seduce. Besides the fact that it was still very new, I was much more comfortable in my independence than I was at the time Charlie and I split. I had hit my stride as a single lady. I figured if things ended, I'd spend a few days whining to Granny and casting spells with my Colombian friend, then forget about him by St. Patrick's Day.

When I asked Granny to weigh in she advised, "Keep dating other men longer than you think you should."

"But I don't even know if *he's* still dating other people."

"Men can smell other men," she declared. "Once they detect the scent or suspect another suitor in the mix, male competitive instincts kick in." I knew Granny was right, and besides, I've always found it safer to operate under the assumption that until a guy tells me he wants to be exclusive, we are *both* free to date whomever we'd like.

In early February, after a two-day dry spell of no word from my friend Nate, I decided to take Granny's advice and keep my dating wheels greased up. I logged back on to How About We and found a date posted by a weirdo named Will that interested me.

Will made me feel excited and intimidated. It wasn't so much because I thought we'd click. It was more because after reading his How About We profile I concluded that the chances he was a psychopath were very good, but that was the reason I was "intrigued" to begin with.

He posted the following dates that caught my eye:

**Date Option 1.** *How about we* . . . go out for drinks and you can listen to me talk about my last relationship. I'll share in detail how we met, the great memories we had, and what led to its downfall. I'll finish by talking about how awful she is and why she has made me a miserable person. If time permits, you can say a few words about yourself.

**Date Option 2.** *How about we* . . . make our own hot toddies at our apartments (or your parents' house if that's where you live) and Skype for a couple hours. That way we can continue to browse HowAboutWe.com for people that we'd actually want to go on dates with AND we can improve on our multi-tasking skills.

**Date Option 3.** *How about we* . . . dress up, head to a park with my buddy Brad, who is a professional photographer, and take engagement photos. We'll then post the photos and update our Facebook relationship status to "engaged" and confuse our friends who didn't even realize we were dating anyone.

His dates made me laugh. I was pretty sure they were jokes, but they were still the most creative ones I had seen on the site. I clicked "intrigued" for the first one. It was sad, honest, and hilarious. I assumed that if nothing else, the date would be interesting.

When online dating, you don't need to always choose guys who you think you'll be attracted to or fall in love with. You can pick guys just to have a laugh, to have an unusual experience, or to experiment with your tastes. No one is forcing you to go out with the eccentrics who you typically wouldn't consider, but I recommend it. You might surprise yourself. And besides, it's better than sitting alone on the couch stalking friends from middle school on your laptop.

I knew the weirdness that I was getting myself into with Will. On his profile he answered:

*For Me, a First Date No-No Is: being serious.*

*What I Would Bring to Show and Tell: 2 dozen mice and a lock for the door.*

*A Story You Should Remind Me to Tell You on Our First Date: I brought two dozen mice to show and tell and locked the door on everyone.*

At his request, I gave him my number and he called. This was the first time I talked on the phone with someone prior to meeting on a date. I know that's typical protocol for many online daters, including Granny, but thus far I had only dealt with men of the twenty-first century who stuck strictly to readable communication (i.e., online messages, emails, texts, and sexts).

Our phone conversation was just as wacky as his date suggestions. I wasn't sure what was sincere and what was bullshit. He played me Rihanna's "We Found Love" through the receiver and asked me if the chorus ("we found love in a hope-less place") reminded me of the dating sites. I was sold.

We grabbed lattes at Think Coffee in Union Square, settling in at a table next to a lesbian couple in the midst of a teary breakup. As soon as we sat down neither of us knew how to react. Our online correspondence had been so bizarre, but the facade immediately dropped when we were face-to-face. There was an awkward introduction and very little eye con-tact until I broke the ice and asked him to please recount the story (fictional or realistic) of his last relationship as he said he would in his How About We date suggestion.

Will nervously laughed then began to get into it. "She slept with my dad . . . and my mom . . . then my brother caught them," he joked, but in person it was hard for him to keep up his schtick. He began to get lost in his story. "Okay," he confessed. "She's actually a very sweet girl. We dated for six years, since high school, but neither of us were ready to get married so we broke up a few months ago."

We both cracked up and dropped our guards. He was clearly very clever and taking the piss out of the dating site, but I was amused. Now that the Band-Aid was peeled back on his ex, he let his theory on relationships flow. I'm sure he didn't actually anticipate talking about his ex with an on-line dating stranger, yet it was a surprisingly liberating exer-cise. We didn't know each other so there were no judgments or long-standing histories to consider. He talked about how when you've had a serious relationship fail at such a young age, it's hard to let yourself be vulnerable and fall for someone again.

I could *totally* relate. His feelings reminded me of where

I was emotionally last year. We think our experiences, heartaches, and hang-ups are unique to us, but in reality they are glaringly universal. I was afraid to let myself truly open up to Nate, only to end up back in heartbreak hotel like I did after Charlie. I had gained so much strength over the past year, putting my breakup behind me, but I still needed to get over the fear of failing again.

I listened as Will explained that he was basically looking for a girl to attend all of his buddies' weddings with and maybe grab a beer or two during the week. He was in the early stages of healing from his split. Commitment seemed to terrify him. Online dating was an attractive alternative for him, an ego boost that helped improve his game in a casual realm.

Will and I crossed into friend territory fast, breaking every first date rule in the book. Although I loved his TMI manner of speaking, it was clear that romantically we were in totally different places. Our "date" oddly made me more aware of the progress I had made and the hopes I was beginning to harbor for the future.

I wasn't the only one recognizing a change in mind-set. Granny was catching the dating fever and learning to embrace the weirdness. Although there were no solid romantic sparks thus far in her dating journey, she was enjoying the opportunity of being in contact with men from all different walks of life, some she could relate to with grandkid or New York chat, others who she was learning from, and, of course, a handful who she couldn't stand. Regardless of how she felt toward them, it was exciting that after more than seven decades on this earth, she was making new connections and still growing.

When Jeff, a lanky masseur, left her a message, she called me ready to trash-talk. "His voice, he's trying to sound sexy and sultry," she purred in a seductive tone. "Give me a break."

"You know nothing about him," I reminded her. "Like you tell me, he might be interesting conversationally rather than sexually."

"He's a masseuse!"

"No, he's a retired lawyer who has taken up massage therapy," I corrected.

"An old man handing out massages, what does that say to you?" she asked.

"He's a man of many talents?"

"No, he'll take a cup and grab however he can get it."

"Why do you have to be so negative?" I pried.

"I'm not negative, honey. I'm a realist. You know that I only give them a tough time because it's more fun. It's defensive pessimism."

"So you're going to have coffee with him?"

"Yes, of course. Cool your jets," she assured me. "And I'm going to have a biscotti too."

Jeff and Granny got to know each other at a café in her neighborhood. After getting the initial bitching out of her system with me, she went into her date much more relaxed than normal. She was coming around to the idea that there was nothing for her to lose. When you're shopping for quantity rather than quality, you spend less time deliberating in your head, *Should I go out with him? Is this a real possibility? What if he doesn't like me?* Instead, you get more comfortable in your dating skin and learn to accept that if something works out, terrific, but if it doesn't, oh well, move on!

"We're cut from different cloths, but he is an exceedingly

interesting man," she told me after their date. She couldn't get over the fact that he'd only visited New York, her stomping ground and life source, once. He asked if she'd ever been to the theater; she said, "Have I ever gone to the theater? Whaddaya crazy? I'm seventy-six. If you're from New York and seventy-six and have never been to the theater, you got some screws loose."

Although she wasn't feeling any romantic vibes, she liked him. "He's spiritual and very smart, a brain, an intellectual," she said, truly surprised. "But he's book smart. I'm not book smart, I'm street smart. We're reversed, you catch my drift? He's unlike anyone I've ever encountered." It's hard to date out of your comfort zone at any age, but it seems especially difficult as you get older. I thought by seventy-six, with all her worldly travels, she would have come across every character in the book.

"Any chance you'll let him massage you?" I teased.

"Yeah sure, I'll let him give me a good rubdown, then I'll be all warmed up to perform my Cirque du Soleil–ish contortion tricks." She then broke out into a fit of giggles.

"Granny!"

"Kid, I will definitely see him again," she assured me. "He was entertaining. I had fun!"

# IRL

VALENTINE'S DAY WAS UPON US. I hate it. I always find that people put too much effort into either glorifying or ignoring the holiday. Even when I was in a relationship with Charlie it was a day I preferred to play down. It all feels too manufactured. I don't even like roses! Dahlias are a different story . . . but still. The best Valentine's Day present I ever got was a necklace with DO ME engraved into it, but even with genuine love of a partner and the thrills of a naughty necklace, I could never get into the holiday.

Of course, I was jaded. I had spent the past five Valentine's Days selling booze in a nightclub. Who do you think goes out to a nightclub on Valentine's Day? Loving couples? No. Warm souls? Think again. Crazy single people who feel they need to overcompensate by celebrating their singledom in full force? Yup.

When I asked Granny if she had any plans for the holiday, she said, "Well, I already ate a brownie and it's not even lunchtime yet. I'd say I'm going all out this year."

Even with my self-enforced dismissal of the holiday, I was curious to see how Nate would handle it. We were seeing each other fairly regularly, so I expected him to at least mention the holiday, only as if to say, "It's Valentine's Day." Or, "Happy Valentine's Day." Or, "I hate Valentine's Day." But the day came and went; he texted me some silly banter and made plans to grab dinner on the fifteenth, but there was no recognition of the Hallmark event. *Aha, so that's how the tall fella from Down Under wants to play it,* I thought. Über denial of cupid's arrow.

In the meantime, my sleazy sensei Robert, the dating junkie, was blowing up my phone with the persistent offer of a post-Valentine drink. Things between us were completely platonic, but it's nice to be surrounded by male energy.

It was the end of winter but I was still lugging around several bulky layers. I stripped down to my blouse and settled in for some gossip. "I have news," he told me over a crystal bowl of booze at Cienfuegos, a colorful cocktail bar on Avenue A.

Although I consider myself a good listener, I am a much better talker. Before I let Robert divulge his gossip, I cut him off and began unloading to him about my recent dates and messages.

I sensed a less ogly vibe from Robert. He was more focused, confident, and seemingly grounded. He hadn't even checked out my cleavage once. Who was this imposter? I narrowed my eyes in on him. "Have you hit a new level on the OkCupid game?" I asked curiously.

He proudly shook his head. "I'm off."

"Is this an attempt at New Year's resolution?" I was suspicious.

He shook his head again.

"You're trying out another site?" I pressed on.

He smiled big. "I met someone. I have a girlfriend."

I was taken aback. Robert had become official with someone before me. Goddamn he was good. When we met almost six months prior, I thought we were both casual daters. He was plowing through the sites like a sport.

"Whoa. You're one of the online dating statistics!" I put my drink down and gave him a dramatic slow clap.

"Not exactly." He smirked. "She's an IRL girlfriend."

"What's that?"

"In real life? You know, that's what the kids say these days," he teased. "We met through friends at a party a few months ago."

"What?" I couldn't help but laugh. "All those online women that you plowed through on the web wasted?"

"Not wasted, they were all helpful in finding me my gal."

"I didn't even think a girlfriend was something you were looking for."

"I don't think I knew what I was looking for until I met her." He smiled the smile of a man in love.

"What's her story?"

"Sophie Labovitch, she's just an all-around great girl. A photographer, super talented," he bragged.

"Did you just tell me her last name because you expect me to google her?"

"Yes." He smirked again.

I obviously googled Sophie, and based off her online footprint, she seemed like a really rad lady.

There's no denying that Robert's tactics were at times trashy, but I was glad he found what he was looking for and couldn't help but believe that online dating played a constructive tool in leading him to her. Although I was psyched for him, I was also partially freaked out for myself that I hadn't sealed any such deal yet. Online dating is not a race, but I have a naturally competitive spirit, and hearing about Robert's big score shook something up inside of me.

Nate and I had been spending a significant amount of time together. We shared a bed at least three nights out of the week, yet we still had not come to verbalize what we were.

I asked myself if being in a relationship with Nate was something that I truly wanted. For my ego, yes, of course I wanted him to want to be with me and only me, but for myself, was I ready? I had put Charlie behind me and spent a fair amount of time exploring my singledom, an important step before engaging in a new relationship, yet I still had hesitations. Nate's bar was getting closer and closer to opening. It felt like an expiration date (even if it was one that I was self-imposing). I needed an excuse to keep my emotions at bay and that was what I chose to cling to.

I was Robert's protégée; he gave me some, at times, questionable but overall solid dating advice. Now that he had proved himself to be capable of locking down a relationship, I began to pry for his opinion on Nate.

"He sounds great. I think you should take it slow and see how things develop," he said in an effort to shut me up. "Your granny is right though—until a man tells you he's just with you, assume that he is not."

"Do you think I should be offended that he consistently refers to me as his 'good friend'?"

"You probably are a good friend. Do you want him to be more than your good friend?"

I considered, although the answer was glaringly clear in my heart. I tried to play it safe. "I *think* so."

"If you're ready to be with someone and this is the guy you want to be with, then you should *know* so."

I was too big of a wimp to admit it out loud, so instead

I poured myself another cocktail from the punch bowl we shared. Fuck, I wanted to be in a relationship with Nate. I had been hanging on to ridiculously superficial things like the fact that he was *too* good-looking (what is wrong with me?!) or my reservations about him opening a bar. He was an ambitious man who was driven enough to start his own business before thirty, and I was a nutcase for projecting my own fears of men onto him. Being around him made me wildly happy, and that's all that really matters.

"Sometimes you just need to let things run their course naturally," Robert advised as he saw the insane internal monologue going on behind my eyes.

"Yep" was all I could manage.

"When the time is right to DTR, you'll know."

"DTR?"

"Define the relationship."

"Aha, I'm glad you were able to DTR with the gal you met IRL," I teased.

# Whole Foods Hookups

B Y SPRING ONE THING became clear: I had created a monster. A man-hunting love monster. I got a call from Granny, and when I picked up she was laughing so hard I could barely understand a word she was saying. Finally she choked out, "Kid, I grew a pair. I did something I wouldn't do in a million years."

She was perusing the aisles of Whole Foods when she came across a case of cheap wine—$2.99 a bottle. She considered buying it—it could make a good gift for her coworkers—but then she asked herself, "Am I that cheap?" I'm pretty sure we both already knew the answer to this.

As she deliberated, a darker-skinned, older man showed up on the scene. "An Arab," she proudly stated in her thick Jewish New Yorker accent.

"A what?" I asked.

"He was an Egyptian, you know like walk like an Egyptian?" she elaborated.

Aha. Got it. So this Egyptian fellow began filling his cart with the wine. Granny took note of this and asked him, "Have you tried this wine before? Do you know if it's any good?"

He scooted his cart closer to her. "In fact I have and I really enjoyed the red," he replied. "But I didn't care for the white."

The two of them began an intelligent conversation about wine until Granny narrowed her eyes in on him and suggestively asked with the skills of a pro detective, "Well, maybe your *wife* enjoys the white?"

He sadly shook his head and explained that his dear wife died six months prior. Now he was a bachelor, a *lonely* bachelor who was confiding his life story to her in the liquor aisle of Whole Foods. She listened and gave her two cents wherever it allowed, then said, "Look, you're a very sad man, and you have every right to be. Let me give you my number; when you're done mourning, call me, we'll go out."

I squealed with delight at her forwardness. What a pro! Where did this dating veteran come from?

She said his eyes lit up as he quickly scrambled to get a pen and paper. "I will, I *definitely* will," he said enthusiastically.

I was impressed and was about to tell her so when she cut me off. "Kid, I got more juice."

After saying good-bye and grabbing the wine, she made her way to the deli counter. "I wanted some roast beef, you know sliced for a sandwich? Whole Foods has beautiful roast beef," she explained. At the counter she caught the eye of another silver-haired gentleman who spontaneously struck up a conversation with her. "I was on a roll, kid, a goddamn roll."

Long after her roast beef had been sliced, she remained talking to this new gentleman when lo and behold the Egyptian returned to the scene. "Thank you so much for your number," he exclaimed. "I'm gonna call you, you're definitely gonna hear from me. I really am looking forward to it."

The silver fox gave Granny a confused look. "He must have thought, 'Is this an old hooker? Does she do this for a profession? A Whole Foods hooker,'" she said, giggling. Completely flustered and overwhelmed by her own mojo, Granny fled the scene. She said bye to both of them, quickly considered scoping out one more aisle to see if she could spot a third suitor, then changed her mind and headed for the check-out counter.

We both laughed hysterically as she recounted the story. "Where did all this sassy chutzpah come from?" I asked.

"The devil made me do it, and kid, you're the devil."

The online practice was affecting Granny offline, and our constant contact meant that our tendencies and sensibilities were rubbing off on each other. For Granny, dating and flirting had become a casual and fun part of her day-to-day life. She was confident, forward, and opening up to new people and different situations.

"What's going on with Ira?" I pried.

"Ira who?" she teased.

"I haven't heard you bring him up in a while. Have you talked to him recently?"

"Yes, a few months ago, but I had nothing to say to him." She laughed. "Been there, done that."

"Really?" I was surprised she had kept their call from me. "How come you didn't mention it earlier?"

"Because that's how insignificant it was. Honey, he's truly history."

"Nothing is going on between you two?" I pushed.

"Kid, we already spent so much of our lives lying about our affair. I'm too old to make shit up now."

"How did you feel when he called you?"

"I felt like I was busy." She giggled. "Because I am!"

It seemed as though Granny had finally rid Ira from her head and heart, freeing up space for whatever or whoever might come next.

# Granny Knows Best

THE YEAR I TURNED twenty-four, my birthday celebration ended at 2 a.m. in a shady Chinese restaurant, where I cried my eyes out, wallowing over past celebrations that I had shared with Charlie. I scarfed down General Tso's chicken and projected far too much meaning on my fortune cookie's prediction. Pathetic. *This* year, my twenty-fifth birthday, those memories were far behind me. I was throwing myself a shindig at Sons of Essex, a new hipsterish venue in my neighborhood. I had a spiffy little blue party dress, and I felt fantastic.

Although we had yet to DTR, as the cool kids say, I invited Nate to my party and encouraged him to bring some buddies along. As I walked into the bar with my friends, I spotted him. He was the first attendee, sitting alone in a corner with a bouquet of flowers in his lap and a big, warm smile on his face. Oh, I was really starting to get addicted to that adorable full-lipped grin of his.

When his friends arrived I greeted one of his pals who I had met previously. He introduced me to another mate as "Kayli, Nate's *girlfriend.*" I laughed nervously, blushed, and made an uncomfortable high-pitched squeal as I shook his friend's hand. Did he know something I didn't?

Rather than overthinking any of it, I danced around, drank tequila, and chowed down on churros. Twenty-five was looking pretty sweet to me. All my friends who were meeting Nate for the first time oohed and aahed. "What's the story? Are you guys together?" they asked. He was there with a dozen roses and his arm around me—for the moment that was all I cared about.

That night Nate waited with me until every guest left the party. Back at my apartment I put his flowers in a vase. He wrapped his lengthy (half-of-six-foot-seven) arm around my waist, pulled me in close, and said, "Beautiful birthday girl, did you have a fun night?" I nodded enthusiastically and went in to kiss him, but before I could stick my tongue down his throat, he pulled back and said, "You know I care about you a helluva lot." I nodded again in a more spastic fashion. Then went back in to shut him up with a kiss. I sabotaged an opportunity to DTR! I am a lady who is rarely short on words, but in that moment, full of churros and cocktails, I didn't know what to say.

To celebrate the first quarter of my life, I went home to Florida to see my family. At the airport I jumped in my mom's car. Before I could get a word in she began gushing about all the changes she'd noticed in Granny. "Kayli, she's nonstop now. Not only is she going on all of these dates, but it feels like every time I turn my head I find her chatting up some silver fox. The supermarket, movie theaters, parking lots—anywhere we go she's making friends with strangers. It's fantastic." She laughed.

I loved that my mom had managed to tap into the excitement of it all too. Poor Mom is typically the monkey in the middle, constantly feeling left out in our shenanigans.

A few weeks before my trip, Granny had been flirting with an old hippie on JDate. Although he lived in South Florida, he wrote to her that he'd been "chilling" with some pals in Cali for the past few weeks but would love to meet up with her upon his return. Based off his profile, where he tells tales of working on a kibbutz, owning vegetarian restaurants, and winning "legendary" tennis competitions, it was clear that this man had led quite a life. But, of course, so has Granny.

"He asked, 'What's the subject of your best story?'" she told me over the phone, clearly entertained.

"What is it?" I asked, expecting her to draw a blank or, at the very least, take a moment to consider.

"Oh, he doesn't want to know," she said, bursting out in a fit of giddy laughter. "Or I don't want to tell him. One or the other."

I was suspicious and envious. How did my seventy-six-year-old granny know off the top of her head the subject of her best story? She's lived fifty years longer than me, had countless more experiences, and yet she automatically knew what it was. If someone asked me that question I'd need time to think and then probably opt for the top five, where at least one tale would involve summer camp.

"What is it?" I asked, brimming with curiosity.

"I'm not going to do this with you now," she whispered in a hushed tone.

"You know *immediately* what the subject of your *best* story is?" I pressed on.

"Yes," she confidently confirmed. "But I'm not going to tell you now. I have *company.*"

"Who?"

"Your mother."

I could hear my mom, who had obviously been eavesdropping, pipe up in the background. "You can tell my daughter, but not me?"

"Because you're *my* daughter. I can tell *your* daughter whatever I want. If you want to know, ask her," Granny said defensively.

"But she never tells me anything." My mom whined loudly enough I could hear it on my end.

"That's because you're her mother."

Ah, the judgmental relationship between a mother and daughter. I love that it skips a generation and I get to be the one swapping salacious secrets with my granny. Regardless, it was nice that all three generations of my family were supportive and excited about our mutual hunt for love.

Catching some rays on the beach with Granny, we got to chatting. "What's the story? Are you in a full-on relationship yet?" she pried.

"I think so." I smiled, pleased to have Nate on my mind.

"What do you mean you *think*? You are or you aren't."

"Well, we haven't had a defining conversation just yet, but I think so."

"Do you want him to be your boyfriend?" she asked.

I nodded and reached for the sunblock that she was forcing in my direction. "You seem hesitant," she persisted, knowing me better than I know myself. "Are you over Charlie?" I nodded. "All the way over Charlie?"

"Yes." I could confidently say I was. "This has been a crazy year. Charlie is behind me but I'm not sure if I'm over the fear of getting hurt again." At the start of our dating journey I was in a dark place; through our little project I had come out of it. I didn't want to risk losing my light.

"Like Roosevelt said, 'We have nothing to fear but fear itself.' You gotta move past that." She grabbed my wrist. "Look at me. Your stubbornness and bullying has gotten me off my tush and back into the game. It's a scary thing at any age but you have to let that go." She was, as always, right. A twenty-five-year-old getting back on the horse is expected, but a seventy-six-year-old is a much bigger deal.

"I know Nate's a great guy, but how do I know if he's the right guy for me?"

"You don't."

"Was that supposed to be comforting?"

"I go back to the old adage that a shrink told me a hundred years ago," she said. "'What you really know is that you *don't* know.' That you can count on."

"My sensei!" I laughed, grasping her hand.

"Kid, you're smart and tough, tougher than me and I'm pretty freaking tough. Just go with it and trust your instincts," she urged. "No one, especially me, is telling you to marry the guy now or ever, but if you're open to being with someone again and this guy is good to you and has the qualities that you want in a man, then quit the heavy analysis and let yourself fall for him. You're ready for the *next* love of your life."

# D to the T to the R

I WAS READY TO TALK SHOP. The night I arrived home in New York, I met up with Nate. Back at his apartment over take-out sushi, I fumbled with my chopsticks, twirling the seaweed salad. Like Robert said, you know when it's time to DTR. Nate's bar was set to open within the month and I didn't care to stick around and play the role of "good friend" to a wildly busy business owner. I was ready to define the relationship.

"I need to talk with you about something," I began. I could feel my face getting flushed with nerves and wasabi spice. As soon as I opened my mouth, I feared I was about to say something that resembled an ultimatum — the last thing I ever want to do is deliver an ultimatum. I paused, trying to carefully articulate the message in my head before I formed the words.

"Yes?" he asked.

By my freaked-out expression, I'm sure he was able to read what was going on in my mind. "So, you and me . . . you and I . . . us—" I paused, trying to gain a touch of composure. "We've been hanging out for a while now."

He nodded, his face also turning red. I grabbed a pillow and held it in front of my head.

"Yes, and well, your bar is opening soon and you're going to be even more busy than you already are, and before that happens—" I gulped.

He pulled down the pillow and gave me an adorable smile. "Are you asking me to be your boyfriend?"

"What? No!" I exclaimed with far too much angst. But yes, that was exactly what I was gearing up for.

"Really?" He set down his chopsticks and came closer to me, smiling. "Because I'd really like to be your boyfriend. Would you like to be my girlfriend?"

"Yes!" I tried to regain my cool. "I mean, yeah, I would. That'd be cool. Sure. I'd like that a lot." We shared a massive raw fish kiss. He admitted that he'd been going through a similar thought process but feared that *I* might have been the one who wasn't ready to commit.

We had been "dating" for almost six months before we settled into a relationship. It was perhaps the most mature and truly intimate beginning I had ever fallen into. When we made the decision to be together, it wasn't just because we wanted to be with someone; we wanted to be with each other. We had put in the time to really get to know each other and were making a commitment that we were both prepared for.

The next morning I did the obvious thing: I called Granny. Although I suspected she'd be excited for me, I considered the chance she might be bummed that we were no longer wingwomen on a shared hunt.

"I have a boyfriend," I told her.

She laughed. "Finally."

"What do you think?"

"I think I love him and I'm crazy about him," she said. "You wanna know why? Because you are and he makes you happy. I'm happy if you're happy, you know that." What a granny.

Before all of our online dating hoopla began, me and Granny, we were of course close—she was my grandmother after all—but through our shared year of bitching and laughing she had become much more than that to me. We're a funny pair. They say the old can't hear and the young don't listen, but as it turns out there's a lot to learn from each other.

Nate's bar opened later that spring. He proudly trotted me around, introducing me to all the staff as "Kayli, my girlfriend, extra VIP," assuaging any lingering fears of the "lewd bar owner" stereotype. Watching him as a leader and hardworking business owner only made him more attractive. He is truly *fantastic*.

He is my Mr. Right, maybe forever or maybe just for this point in my life. Who knows what next month, next year, the next decade, or the rest of my life will bring. You can only live life in the moment, learn to love yourself and love those who love you back. Like Granny says, "What you really know is that you *don't* know." No one knows what the future holds, but if you trust your gut, know who you are, fall in love, allow yourself to fail, accept it, but then *move on*, you *will* love again.

Online dating brought us out of shells of self-pity and past memories. It forced us to move forward and learn more than we expected about each other and ourselves. Granny was still single, but a much more open and forward single than a year prior, and not giving up looking for fun and new experiences. I, however, was out of the game. Luckily Granny's advice is not limited to the one-hit-wonder world of dating. The lady can dole it out in heavy scoops for full-on relationships too.

# Acknowledgments

I am grateful to so many people for so many reasons. First off, Granny, thank you for your patience, enthusiasm, and encouragement in this book and everything else in my life.

Mom, thanks for making me, being my mom, and introducing me to your mom.

Danielle, thanks for being a role model in online dating and everything else under the sun. There's a good reason for your "favorite granddaughter" title.

Thank you to the folks at Levine and Greenberg, especially Daniel Greenberg for believing in the story.

At Amazon, thank you to Katie Salisbury for all of the crucial guidance and everyone who helped make this book what it is.

To Laurel Pantin, thanks for being the biggest bean on the block, getting me drunk, and convincing me twice to get matching tattoos, and for helping me edit this book.

To my friends, holy shit, I love you. Melissa Vargas, thank you for a million things. Men are great, but you are better. Tina Imm, Katherine Grainger, Simone Ross, Catherine Kelly,

Leba Haber, Victoria Wellman, Julia Hanley, Gayla Hibner, Henry-Alex Rubin, Christina Cochran, Jason Mantzoukas, Matt Taback, Tom Calderone, Pippa Bianco, Rose Lockwood, Cristina Silva, Meaghan Oppenheimer, Jessie Stollak, Joel Veach, Kara Stemle, Noah Wunsch, Daphne Lim and everyone else in my life, thank you, thank you, thank you!

To the men who have kindly taken the time to date me, I have learned so much from all of you. Thanks for putting up with me.

Kayli Stollak is a writer living in
the Lower East Side of New York City.